50 OBJECTS FROM VINDOLANDA

Barbara Birley and Elizabeth M. Greene

AMBERLEY

First published 2024

Amberley Publishing
The Hill, Stroud
Gloucestershire, GL5 4EP

www.amberley-books.com

Copyright © Barbara Birley and Elizabeth M. Greene, 2024

The right of Barbara Birley and Elizabeth M. Greene to be identified as the Authors of this work has been asserted in accordance with the Copyrights, Designs and Patents Act 1988.

ISBN 978 1 3981 1658 0 (print)
ISBN 978 1 3981 1659 7 (ebook)

British Library Cataloguing in Publication Data.
A catalogue record for this book is available from the British Library.

Typeset in 10pt on 13pt Celeste.
Typesetting by SJmagic DESIGN SERVICES, India.
Printed in the UK.

Contents

Acknowledgements

We would like to thank everyone, including the trustees, staff and volunteers at the Vindolanda Trust for their help and support for this project. Special thanks are extended to Rob Sands, Mark Hoyle and Mike Bishop for use of their images and drawings in the publication. If not noted, the illustrations are the copyright of the Vindolanda Trust, and thanks must go out to Sonya Galloway and Penny Trichler for their additional photographic skills. Proofreading and editing thanks go to Andrew Birley, Alexander Meyer and Ann Hetherington. We would also like to acknowledge a number of friends and colleagues within the wider Romano-British scholarly community for their help and support of ongoing research on the Vindolanda collection over many years including Marta Alberti, Lindsay Allason-Jones, Anthony Birley, Mike Bishop, Alan Bowman, Rob Collins, Carol van Driel-Murray, Craig Harvey, Alex Mullen, Rob Sands, David Thomas, Roger Tomlin and J. P. Wild. Further thanks are extended to Andrew Birley for his help with archaeological contexts, and to both Andrew and Alexander Meyer for their encouragement throughout. This book would not have been possible without the lifetime commitment to the excavation, conservation, and research of the Vindolanda site by Robin and Patricia Birley. We dedicate this book to them. Financial support for this project was provided by the Vindolanda Trust, the Canada Research Chairs Program (Award: CRC-2019-00113), the Social Science Humanities Research Council Canada, and the University of Western Ontario.

Foreword

The site of Roman Vindolanda is truly a remarkable place. Situated in the rolling hills of Northumberland alongside the Roman road known as the Stanegate, it lies only a mile to the south of the later line of Hadrian's Wall. A succession of timber forts built here gradually gave way to buildings in stone, which effectively sealed the remains of the earlier forts from the air we breathe today and protected their remains from later disturbances. This created an almost unrivalled archaeological preservation landscape in which a broad range of objects and architecture survived for thousands of years preserved in the Vindolanda mud, when elsewhere they would turn into the soil that surrounds them. Roman shoes, textiles, basketry, and other organics have been preserved alongside wooden artefacts that are so incredibly fragile, like the thin ink-on-wood letters, that it is astounding that they should be preserved for us to recover and read today.

The excavations at the site, conducted by the Vindolanda Trust over a fifty-year period and led by professional archaeologists with teams of dedicated hard-working volunteers, has reshaped our appreciation of what it meant to be a Roman soldier serving in Britain. Because of some of the extraordinary finds from the site, we have a much clearer idea of who one might have met in a Roman fort or military town 2,000 years ago.

The work of condensing the many thousands of Vindolanda artefacts into fifty of the most remarkable finds that have come from the site is a monumental task undertaken by the authors, Barbara Birley and Elizabeth M. Greene. What they show is that each object profiled here, whether magnificent or mundane, takes us on a journey to a time and place which is now a little less alien to us, thanks to the common humanity which bonds the fifty artefacts together. Each was held, created, traded, written, loved, or lost by a human hand and by marveling at and enjoying those things today we better appreciate the people to whom they once belonged.

Dr Andrew Birley
CEO of The Vindolanda Trust

Chapter 1
The Roman Fort at Vindolanda, the Army, and the Soldiers

The site of Vindolanda was defined by the presence of the Roman army for well over 300 years, from the late first century CE to the end of Roman occupation in the fifth century. The site continued to be a centre of shifting power in the region even after this point, with significant evidence for settlement in the sub- and post-Roman phases. The very first Roman occupation on the site occurred in around CE 85, when a fort was constructed to house a cohort of nominally 500 men. Archaeological evidence from this earliest period of occupation suggests that women and children were also present in the settlement at this time, so we must imagine a thriving community with the military unit and dependents of the soldiers living in and around the fort. The earliest phases of occupation at Vindolanda between CE 85 and CE 120 saw a series of timber forts, each one bigger than its predecessor, to house the growing size of the military units stationed on-site.

Vindolanda was part of the defensive line established in the late first century CE on the north-west frontier of the Roman empire, now called the Stanegate. A series of forts dotted the landscape at this time and were connected at some point by a road and communications system. Vindolanda is located in the centre of this defensive line and held what must have been a strategic location near natural resources and communication nodes. During the period leading up to the construction of Hadrian's Wall in the CE 120s, Vindolanda was occupied by its largest unit, the First Cohort of Tungrians, who were housed in the biggest fort ever to be built on-site, which extends much farther to the west than its predecessors. Vindolanda remained occupied during the construction, occupation, abandonment and re-occupation of Hadrian's Wall, and seems to have played an important role in the staging of Wall construction. During Period 4 at Vindolanda, very large store houses and other features on-site point to its role in the dynamic activity of the region at this time. Vindolanda continued to house Roman auxiliary units, as well as the large contingent of non-combatants that inevitably grew around a military fort through the second, third, and fourth centuries. The forts changed from timber construction to stone during the second century and the substantial remains of the third-century stone fort and large settlement to its west still stand today on display for site visitors. Several additions and adaptations of this latest fort are clear in the archaeological record and by the fourth and fifth centuries the site was furnished with apsidal buildings that appear to be early churches. There is evidence for occupation of the site through the sixth or seventh centuries and some artefacts suggest activity still in the ninth century. After being abandoned, the site remained unexplored for hundreds of years until its rediscovery and excavation in the nineteenth and twentieth centuries.

The archaeology and the objects from Vindolanda are quite exceptional because the early periods of occupation, between c. CE 85 and CE 130, sit in oxygen-reduced environments (anaerobic or anoxic), which preserve organic finds extraordinarily well. Discovery and excavation of these important archaeological contexts began in the 1970s by Robin Birley and the excavations on the site have continued to produce unique and exceptional objects over the past five decades. Today a thriving international team of professional archaeologists, volunteers, and students works on the site every summer to reveal the archaeology beneath. Because of the anaerobic environments found at Vindolanda, the following chapters highlight a number of objects of wood, leather, bone, and textile that are usually not preserved in typical archaeological conditions. The leather and wood collections are some of the best from anywhere in the Roman empire and form one of the great highlights today of visiting the site and museum at Vindolanda, as well as the Roman Army Museum at nearby Carvoran (Roman Magna). What is represented in this book is only the tip of the iceberg and there is so much more for any visitor to explore. These collections are also invaluable for researchers of the Roman army and military communities because the picture of life in the past is so much more complete due to the preservation of organic remains. We are offered an exceptional view of life as a Roman soldier and of the objects that made up the activities and preoccupations of a Roman military unit garrisoning the frontier. From official documents to weapons and armour, as well as leather boots and shoes, the extraordinary collection at Vindolanda offers a robust picture of life at this military settlement during Roman occupation nearly 2,000 years ago.

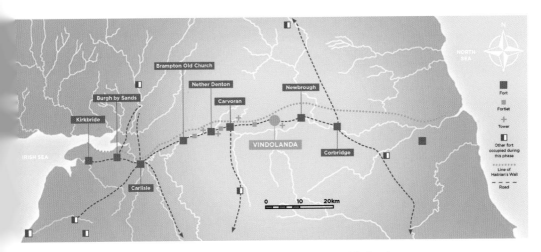

Map of the line of the Stanegate Road with Vindolanda highlighted.

Aerial view of Vindolanda site in spring 2023.

Above left: Robin Birley excavating the early wooden forts in the 1970s.

Above right: Students from University of Western Ontario working on the excavations.

1. Military strength report (*Tab. Vindol.* 154)
Vindolanda Period 1 (*c.* CE 85–90)
Found in a defensive ditch of the earliest fort
Height: 394mm; Width: 86mm

Some of the very best evidence for understanding life in the Roman army has emerged from the discovery of hundreds of wooden writing tablets from the early periods of occupation at Vindolanda. The millimetre-thick sheets of wood were treated and written upon with ink to preserve everything from the status of the military stores or a request for more beer to the personal letters between officers' wives living on the Roman frontier. The Vindolanda strength report is one of the most important documents in the collection to provide a sense of the daily operations of the Roman army in occupied territory. The document reports the total strength of the First Cohort of Tungrians while they occupied the first fort built at Vindolanda. The information offered is incomparable; we learn the number of soldiers that were absent from the fort on detachment duties and the number present, followed by how many soldiers were sick, wounded, and in its own category were those unavailable for service because of eye maladies. The total number of active soldiers was provided at the end.

It seems that all military units across the empire had some sort of daily, monthly, and yearly reporting systems, but that there were variations in the form these might take. Similar documents are known from sites across the empire, especially in Egypt and from Dura-Europos in Syria, where other military forts were located. The Vindolanda document has some unique features and appears to be a strength report offered to the commanding officer for his daily use and perhaps for composing a more formal monthly or yearly report (*pridianum*) at a later stage. Surprisingly, the Vindolanda strength report reveals that out of the official unit strength of 752 men, only 265 were fit for duty at the moment of writing this report. This one thin piece of wood changed our entire image of the occupation of a frontier fort.

Ink-on-wood writing tablet recording a military strength report.

2. Leather marching boot (L-2019-6)
Vindolanda Period 3 (*c.* CE 100–105)
Found in the northern defensive fort ditch
Length: 270mm; Width: 110mm; Height: 114mm

While the strength report gives us a bird's-eye view of the unit as a whole, the thousands of shoes left behind at Vindolanda offer a personal and individual connection with the soldiers and people who once lived on the site. The most ubiquitous shoe type in the leather assemblage is the hardy military boot, dubbed the 'Fell Boot' by Carol van Driel-Murray, to remind one of the landscape and terrain around Vindolanda. The boot seen here replaced the impractical (and perhaps out of style) military marching boot known as the *caliga*, a word that was so closely associated with the Roman army that it was used by Latin authors metonymically to denote the body of soldiers. In the north of Britain, however, the conditions were much better suited to a closed shoe such as the Fell Boot and this footwear type certainly took over from the delicate open-worked boots preferred earlier in the first century CE. Everything about this boot suggests practicality over fashion: the thick closed leather to protect the foot, the many layers of leather used to build up a robust walking sole, and the closely packed lines of iron hobnails on the outer sole to create a sturdy surface for each step. The uppers of this style of boot are also found separated from their shoe sole, seen in the image at the foot of the page (L-2001-55). This shoe type remained a popular style for a very long time after its introduction.

The practical and
sturdy Roman Fell Boot.

Example of Fell Boot
uppers (L-2001-55).

3. Medusa *phalera* (SF-23876)
Vindolanda Period 4 (*c.* CE 105–120)
Found in a storeroom structure inside the fort
Diameter: 59.82mm; Depth: 5.44mm

Soldiers probably valued the decorative elements of their kit as much as the practical armour, especially an object of silver such as this one. This silver *phalera*, a medal or award for distinguished action, depicts the head of the gorgon Medusa. *Phalerae* were sculpted disks made of gold, silver, copper-alloy or glass. The depiction of Medusa is not unusual on *phalerae* generally. Medusa was often favoured in this sort of decoration because of the apotropaic symbolism that hoped to avert evil spirits. In Greek and Roman mythology, Medusa was one of three monstrous sisters known as the Gorgons. She is usually represented as a winged female with a head of live snakes in place of hair. Her gaze was said to turn people to stone. According to the myth, Medusa was slain by Perseus and her severed head was placed on the shield of Athena, giving her the ability to turn enemies to stone. The soldiers wearing images like this *phalera* could have known the meaning of the myth, giving the iconography a power over enemies and acting as a device for their own safety. This *phalera* was at some point repurposed into a brooch, suggesting it held great value to its owners through time.

Silver Medusa *phalera* found in 2023.

4. Pompeii-type *gladius* (SF-21269)
Vindolanda Period 4 (*c.* CE 105–120)
Found in a cavalry barrack of the First Cohort of Tungrians
Length: 720mm; Width: 50mm

The soldiers stationed at Vindolanda had a whole array of weaponry at their disposal. The Vindolanda collection holds many objects that illustrate this and some of the more frequent finds are iron artillery projectile points and *pilum* spear heads. Rarer are the larger finds that we might expect a soldier to guard quite closely. In 2017, the excavations revealed a beautifully preserved Roman sword that was examined by Marta Alberti and Mike Bishop. The blade is complete and made of iron. It is diamond-sectioned in shape and it tapers slightly to a triangular tip. It is known as a Pompeii-type *gladius* (a Latin word for 'sword') and there are very similar examples from Newstead in Scotland and Mainz in Germany. This was the standard type of infantry sword in the first and second centuries and was used as both a slashing and stabbing weapon. It was excavated from a period when the First Cohort of Tungrians and a detachment of Vardulli Cavalry from northern Spain were stationed at Vindolanda. During excavations in the same year, another sword was found (SF-21183) in an adjacent barrack, and was identified as a cavalry *spatha*, the longer sword used by the mounted riders. It is an incomplete iron sword but retains some key components: the ovoid pommel and tubular hand grip fashioned from wood, and parts of the scabbard made of very thin wood. These objects were left behind in the cavalry barrack along with several other very fine objects of bronze, suggesting the unit may have left Vindolanda in a hurry.

Volunteer excavator Sarah Baker with the sword just after discovery.

The Pompeii-type *gladius* (top) and cavalry *spatha* on display at Vindolanda (bottom; SF-21183).

5. Archer's leather finger guard (L-1994-4164)
Vindolanda Period 1 (*c.* CE 85–90)
Found in the bottom fill layer of the defensive fort ditch
Finger cover: *c.* 60mm × 50mm

A different sort of equipment is found in the leather assemblage, where items that are either unique or quite rare add to our understanding of the range of Roman military equipment that existed. A surprise find during excavations in the 1990s by Robin Birley was an archer's finger guard, complete with straps and laces to attach the equipment to one's wrist. The importance of this object to the health and wellbeing of an archer cannot be underestimated. Repeated use of archery equipment can result in damage to the fingers pulling the strings, which could create an uncomfortable and potentially dangerous raw patch over time. The solution is this thin layer of leather that covers the fingers to give a layer of protection and strength for pulling the bowstring. The guard was designed with long leather straps to tie this invaluable piece of equipment to the wrist, allowing it to stay in place better and to prevent its loss when not in use.

Another piece of leather equipment rarely glimpsed is the slinger's pouch (L-1991-3167) found in a Period 6 context (*c.* CE 140–160). The small pocket of thick leather is pinched at both ends to take the string and it used small, lead sling bullets like those seen in the image here. The pouch is also highly decorated on its outside surface, suggesting that military equipment can be both practical and beautiful.

Archer's leather finger guard on display at the Roman Army Museum.

Leather slinger's pouch with decorated surface (L-1991-3167).

Collection of lead sling bullets from Vindolanda.

This unique object, made of juniper haircap moss (*polytrichum juniperinum*), was found sitting among other organic debris in the bottom of a ditch protecting the first fort at Vindolanda. The object is incredibly fragile. Upon arrival in the on-site laboratory the object was examined by Patricia Birley. The presumed helmet crest was made from approximately 2,240 strands of hair moss which were folded in half to form an elongated 'U' shape. It was made of bundles of approximately ten 'hairs' or strands which were folded and then stitched together at the folded end using a four-strand twist of moss. These sewn bundles were then folded in half to produce a bushier effect. It appears that all the strands were approximately 23cm long, but they were then trimmed with scissors or a very sharp knife, leaving longer strands standing tall in the centre of the crest, with graduated trimming to taper to 10cm each side. The strong sewn edge of the crest formed an excellent base for securing it into a crest holder before attaching it to a helmet.

The moss is a perennial species of a type that can still be found growing in the high, woody areas around the site at Vindolanda. The plant produces long, tough, slender 'hairs' which are flexible, reddish in colour, and have the appearance of horsehair. Hair moss is an excellent weaving material and was also used to produce the hair-moss wig, another of Vindolanda's top finds (Object 24).

Hair-moss helmet crest found in the bottom of the fort ditch.

Chapter 2
Women and Children at Vindolanda

Our knowledge of the extended communities surrounding Roman military garrisons has expanded enormously in the past few decades, and Vindolanda has played a significant role in these new discoveries. Substantial communities that included wives, children, parents, and other relatives of soldiers were attached to the military. Women and children of all ranks and statuses were present in military communities, from the wives of elite officers to the enslaved individuals that were part of military households. Their lived experiences differed enormously depending on their status, which must be remembered when we discuss the presence and role of women and children anywhere in antiquity.

There has been significant debate about whether women and children lived inside the forts themselves or only outside in the extramural settlement (the *vicus*). Vindolanda has made many important contributions to these investigations with some of the evidence presented in this chapter. It is quite clear that the family of the commanding officer in Period 3 lived in the *praetorium* (commanding officer's residence) and was part of the everyday life of the fort. Evidence in the form of leather footwear from a Period 4 barrack suggests that women and children may also have lived inside these spaces. Evidence for the residence of women and children inside forts does not appear everywhere, but this may be attributed to the exceptional preservation found at Vindolanda. Most of the evidence for habitation by women and children is found in organic objects of wood and leather, which are not preserved in most archaeological environments. The Vindolanda evidence is exceptional in the world of archaeology today, but it is likely these were common objects in the ancient world that could have been seen in almost all settlements in the Roman period. If shoes and letters were preserved at all military forts our picture of the population might be very different.

Tombstone of Licinia Flavilla and Sextus Adgennius Macrinus from modern Nîmes, France. (Stéphane Ramillon/Ville de Nîmes)

7. The birthday invitation (*Tab. Vindol.* 291)
Vindolanda Period 3 (*c.* CE 100–105)
Found in the bonfire site with records from the *praetorium* of Flavius Cerialis
Width: 223mm; Height: 96mm

Arguably the most emotive piece of evidence revealing the lives of elite women on the northern frontier is the writing tablet known as the 'Birthday Invitation'. The letter was written by Claudia Severa, the wife of the commanding officer at a nearby fort called Briga (location unknown), inviting her friend Sulpicia Lepidina, the wife of Flavius Cerialis (unit commander at Vindolanda) to her birthday celebrations on 11 September. The letter includes a personal greeting at the end written by Claudia Severa herself, 'I shall expect you, sister. Farewell, sister, my dearest soul, as I hope to prosper, and hail' (Bowman & Thomas 1994) that shows the deep friendship between these military wives. The letter also tells us something about the daily lives of the women attached to the elite officers in the unit and shows that they socialised with families of the same status and had some freedom to move around the frontier. This notion of travel for these women is corroborated by another letter between the two women reporting that Severa was given permission to visit Lepidina at Vindolanda whenever she would like (*Tab. Vindol.* 292). These letters reveal an incredible level of freedom and agency on the part of elite military wives, an aspect of military life that had not been considered before this evidence emerged. The importance of family life to the men and women stationed on the frontier was clearly on display throughout the letters in the form of greetings to wives, children, brothers, sisters, and fellow countrymen.

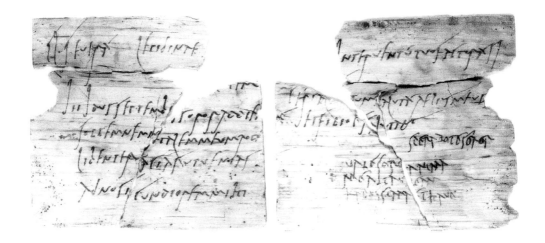

Ink-on-wood writing tablet recording the letter between Sulpicia Lepidina and Claudia Severa.

8. Lepidina sandal (L-7/SF-863)
Vindolanda Period 3 (*c.* CE 100–105)
Found in the *praetorium* of Flavius Cerialis
Length: 215mm; Width: 64mm; Height: 17mm

The 'Lepidina sandal' is one of the finest leather shoes in the Vindolanda collection. Its name derives from the space in which it was found – the Period 3 *praetorium* – which was the residence of Sulpicia Lepidina and her husband Flavius Cerlialis, the commanding officer of the Ninth Cohort of Batavians stationed at Vindolanda. The letters found there, such as the 'Birthday Invitation' discussed above, tell us about the highest-ranking family on-site at this time. The shoe was found near other examples of very fine footwear of the children and adolescents of this family, such as the baby's boot also pictured here (L-1985-67). These shoes are some of the earliest evidence that made it quite clear that the commanding officer's family accompanied him into the military and was in residence inside the fort itself. The sandal was prominently marked by its maker, Lucius Aebutius Thales, making this one of the first 'designer' labels in history. The sandal is incredibly fine and detailed, with individual toes cut out for decorative effect, impressed stamps of floral motifs, and fine incised lines around the edges. The shoe is of great fascination to museum visitors for its similarity to shoe styles today and its pristine preservation after 2,000 years in the ground. It is equally interesting for archaeologists and researchers because of its ability to shed light on the presence of women and children in Roman military communities and to help us better understand this part of the population of military settlements.

Right: The 'Lepidina sandal' from the Period 3 *praetorium*.

Below left: Detail of the maker's mark and leaf stamp on the insole of the 'Lepidina sandal' (L-7/SF-863).

Below right: The baby's boot from the Period 3 *praetorium* (L-1985-67).

9. Gold and green glass earring (SF-2470)
Vindolanda Period 7 (*c.* CE 213–275)
Found in a structure in the extramural settlement
Height: 34mm; Width: 11mm; Depth: 5mm

Fashion can take many forms and the variety is apparent in much of the jewellery found at Vindolanda, especially that probably worn by women. The diverse collection includes eight earrings, the majority of which are made of gold, a precious and limited material found in only a few other objects across the site. The most elaborate earring from the collection is the gold object shown here with a faux emerald bead made of green glass. It has an additional dangling wire with a space for another bead, now missing. In comparison with many surviving earrings from the empire and depictions on stone and mummy portraits from the Fayum region in Egypt, the Vindolanda example is somewhat simple. It is unclear if this is because of taste or means of the owner, but it is generally believed that women of the Roman period, especially those in the western provinces, were probably the owners of such objects instead of their male counterparts. Sculpture and other iconographic media from around the Roman world show decoration on display, as it is in the example of a grave stele of a Palmyran woman from Syria in the eastern empire seen at the foot of the page.

Gold earring with faux emerald bead made of green glass.

Grave stele of a well-adorned woman from Palmyra in Syria. (National Museum of Antiquities, Leiden)

10. Betrothal medallion (SF-258)
Vindolanda Period 6B (*c*. CE 200–212)
Found in an alley beside the commanding officer's residence
Diameter: 2.45mm

Betrothal, or formal engagement for marriage, must have been an important part of Roman life for women on the frontier. This pendant dates to the late third century CE when jet was in fashion, and probably served as a betrothal or marriage gift. Tokens were given to the intended in the form of pendants or rings. This jet pendant is carved on both sides and shows a man and a woman kissing on the front and on the reverse depicts clasped hands (*dextrarum iunctio*), a Roman symbol of the marriage agreement. Jet pendants are usually oval in shape and have a tube at the upper edge for suspension. There are only about two dozen or so known from the empire with the majority of these coming from Britain, including six from Roman York. They depict gorgon heads, mythical scenes and portraits, as well as another betrothal medallion.

Jet was mined and worked on the North Yorkshire coast during the Roman occupation of Britain and came into fashion during the late second to early third century CE. It is likely that the jet found at Vindolanda comes from this area. Jet is known for its deep black colour and its high-gloss surface. Many jet beads, finger rings, and fragments of bangles have been found on the site, and one of the best examples is the complete jet bangle pictured below (SF-376).

Right: Jet medallion with image of a betrothal scene.

Below left: Complete jet bangle from the third century (SF-376).

Below right: Collection of jet beads from Vindolanda.

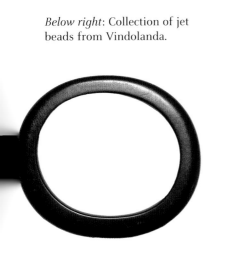

11. Wooden needle case (SF-3917)
Vindolanda Period 2 (*c.* CE 90–100)
Found in Rooms H–I of the proposed Period 2 *praetorium* structure inside the fort
Lid: 91mm × 22mm; Inner portion: 104mm × 22mm

The activities that may have occupied women at the fort can be traced through many of the objects found on-site. This wooden needle case contained several graded iron needles when excavated. Objects like this were presumably fairly common in the ancient world and others like it have been found at Vindolanda (W-1991-954). The collection also holds hundreds of needles recovered during excavations. Bone and tiny iron needles would have been used for all types of sewing, while the fine metal examples could also be used for medical purposes.

The production of cloth, including carding, spinning, and weaving fibres, is illustrated in the objects found on-site, particularly hundreds of spindle whorls and many loom weights. The collection also has several weaving combs made of wood and antler like the one seen opposite (W-1987-258). They were used to push down the spun wool when it was

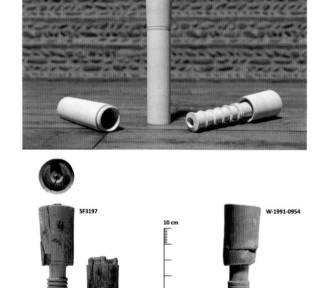

SF3197

10 cm

W-1991-0954

Wooden needle case originally found with metal needles included. (R. Sands)

Wooden comb for weaving
activities (W-1987-258).
(R. Sands)

1 cm

W1987-0258

Two fragments of textile
which have been sewn
together as a possible repair
(TT-1985-25).

0   10 cm

on the loom. The activities associated with cloth production were often seen as women's work and, depending on social status, would have taken place in the home. The people of Vindolanda undoubtedly wore both colourful clothes as well as those woven from undyed natural wools. Many of the surviving textile examples have been examined by J. P. Wild, who noted the great variation in the quality of the textiles found at Vindolanda. Sheep were raised on Roman farms along the frontier and wool was acquired from local farms through taxation. The dyes used in textile production include the root of the madder plant, which produces a red dye. Excavations have also produced a fragment of checked cloth with traces of a lichen-based purple dye (see Object 20). Yellows were possible using a variety of local barks, lichen, and heathers, while adding a rusty nail during the dyeing process could produce a greenish hue. Dyes were set using a mineral alum.

12. Adolescent's pair of shoes (L-1992-3775 and L-1992-3776)
Vindolanda Period 6A (c. CE 160–200)
Found in a construction foundation deposit
Length: 195mm; Width: 65mm; Height: 60mm

The children and adolescents that lived at Vindolanda are best revealed by the hundreds of shoes that were once worn and discarded on-site. Children's shoes are found in all contexts, from internal building spaces to fort ditches, and from all periods of occupation. Some of the best-preserved shoes, like the baby's boot discussed above (see Object 8), conjure images of the real people who inhabited these spaces. A few pairs of children's and adolescents' shoes were discarded or intentionally left behind together and found near each other in excavations. The pair of shoes shown here probably belonged to someone perhaps in their early teen years. These low shoes were a standard type found throughout the north-west empire and have small details such as the pointed leather above the lace holes and some further detail added with stitching.

Another pair of children's shoes from the Severan-period fort ditch (early third century CE) links us to the children and families that lived on-site during periods of potential conflict and upheaval (L-2016-389 and L-2016-438). We are also aware of the children that lived at Vindolanda through one of only a few socks that survive from Roman contexts anywhere in the empire (TT-1987-316). This small sock is made from woven wool and could have been worn inside almost any of the hundreds of children's shoes found on the site. Its suitability for the cold and wet climate of Britain makes it an exciting object to consider the practical side of daily life at Vindolanda.

Above left: Pair of ankle-height shoes belonging to an adolescent.

Above right: Pair of child's shoes from the Severan-period ditch (L-2016-389 and L-2016-438).

Left: Textile sock of a child or adolescent (TT-1987-316).

24

The social expectations of children, especially boys, might be revealed by some of the smaller military objects that have been found on-site. A wooden sword that may have been used as a toy or practice weapon by a child living at Vindolanda emerged from the bottom of a defensive ditch of the earliest period of occupation. The sword is light and could have been easily wielded by a small child. It may also have been used as a practice weapon for an adult, though the light weight and absence of any weighted material such as lead makes one question its practicality for an adult. A similar object was found associated with the occupation of the Period 2–3 fort (*c.* CE 90–105). A small wooden dagger (W-2001-89) was found in the layers of laminate flooring in a building inside the fort. We can only speculate about the social function of such objects, but it is tempting to associate wooden weapons with the young boys who grew up with the Roman army training for their own military careers. Practice weapons could have been enjoyed by boys or girls, but the socialisation of the two groups would have looked quite different, and it is probable that objects related to the military world were not part of girlhood in this context.

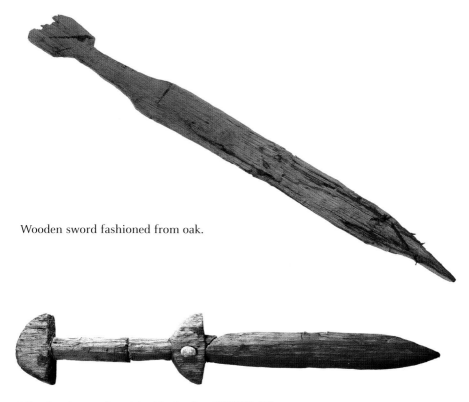

Wooden sword fashioned from oak.

Wooden dagger found inside the fort (W-2001-89).

Chapter 3
Religion and Worship in Roman Military Communities

One of the most important aspects of life at a Roman military fort was the daily expression of religion and spiritual belief. Most of the Roman world operated within a polytheistic system that allowed for the integration of different religious perspectives and the syncretisation of Roman and non-Roman deities. At a site such as Vindolanda, where soldiers were predominantly non-Roman citizens and hailed from the conquered provinces of the empire, we should expect to find evidence for worship outside the typical Greco-Roman sphere. At the same time, there was a distinct military religion that took hold and became strikingly uniform across the empire. In almost every fort a small area called the 'shrine of the standards' (*aedes principiorum*) held the important signs and symbols of the military unit. Every *principia* (headquarters building) also housed the obligatory dedications to the Roman deities most important to the continued success of the army and empire, especially Jupiter Optimus Maximus.

Cults such as those that worshipped Mithras or Jupiter Dolichenus were particularly popular in military environments, possibly because they had the perfect structure of officials and participants in which to reinforce the important hierarchy of the Roman army itself. At Vindolanda, a space to worship Jupiter Dolichenus (a *Dolichenum*) was found inside the third-century fort, complete with altars and other paraphernalia of the cult.

The Romano-Celtic temple in the extramural settlement at Vindolanda, located to the west of the stone forts.

Aerial photograph of the *Dolichenum* situated in the northern rampart of Stone Fort 2 at Vindolanda.

The third-century *praetorium* with an apsidal structure, probably a church, built into its courtyard during later reconstruction. (Photographer: Aerial-Cam)

Alongside the expected deities associated with the Roman army, we also find evidence for the continued worship of deities from the soldiers' homelands. Many forts along Hadrian's Wall have evidence for the worship of deities with Germanic and other north-western European origins. Some soldiers brought their systems of belief from even farther afield and one of the most interesting inscriptions on Hadrian's Wall comes from Magna, a fort 7 miles to the west of Vindolanda, where a Syrian unit was stationed and worshipped a Syrian goddess (*RIB* 1791 and 1792). Other deities were thought to bring fecundity and good luck to the unit or individual, such as Bonus Eventus, Priapus, or Fortuna. Vindolanda also housed a temple in a very typical Romano-Celtic style, pictured here. Eventually, the influence of Christianity became prominent. Vindolanda, where a proposed Christian church was built into the courtyard of the *praetorium,* has played an important role in understanding the emergence of the new religion in the north of England.

14. Altar to Jupiter Dolichenus (SF-13600)
Vindolanda Periods 7–8 (*c.* third–fourth century CE)
Found inside the *Dolichenum* shrine built into the north rampart of Stone Fort 2
Height: 1.5m; Width: .49m; Depth: .48m

The cult of Jupiter Dolichenus was popular within military circles around the empire in the second and third centuries CE, but it was not exclusively a military cult. It was understood to have emerged from Doliche in an area of Asia Minor called Commagene. However, Dolichenus' conflation with Roman Jupiter and the cult's subsequent dissemination throughout the empire makes it difficult to discern its original features from what it became as an amalgamated product of the Roman empire. The worship of Jupiter Dolichenus was known as a 'mystery cult' because of its need for initiation into its ranks, leaving little information about the structure and operation of cult practice and making it necessary to fill in the details with evidence from around the empire. Vindolanda has produced one of the only spaces for its worship located inside the walls of a military fort (pictured on p. 27). The altar pictured here was one of three that were found associated with the small shrine dedicated to cult worship. Another object found discarded nearby, a bronze hand (SF-21515) slightly smaller than life size, also has associations with the cult and was likely a part of worship in the shrine.

 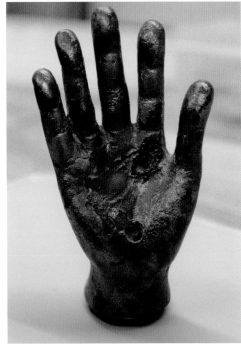

Above left: The front inscription and side carving on the altar to Jupiter Dolichenus. (Photographer: Aerial-Cam)

Above right: The bronze 'hand of god' found near the *Dolichenum* (SF-21515).

15. Inscription to the goddess Ahvardua (SF-4952)
Vindolanda Period 4 (c. CE 105–120)
Found in the northern defensive fort ditch
Length: 480mm; Width: 320mm; Depth: 105mm

One of the most surprising stone inscriptions that demonstrates the variety of religious worship that could be found on the northern frontier was that dedicated to Ahvardua, a deity previously unknown anywhere in the Roman world. She seems to have connections to the homeland of the First Cohort of Tungrians, the unit responsible for the dedication, in northern Gaul and was transported into the military environment at Vindolanda. Ahvardua was a water goddess and her name has elements of old Celtic. The inscription was written in Latin by the Tungrian dedicators to read: 'To the Goddess Ahvardua, the Tungrians...'. The connection to water may be associated with numerous springs located in the vicinity that were in use for an extended period of time. The stone may also have had some relationship with the small Romano-Celtic temple sitting just 8 metres to the west of the main spring (pictured above). This object clearly demonstrates the attachments to the homeland felt by at least some of the Tungrian soldiers, which is often expressed in private spheres of one's life, such as religion and the household. Other objects have similar associations, including a small statue of Fortuna found nearby, that has visual attributes associated with other representations of the goddess from north-western Europe (SF-6772).

Partial inscription to the goddess Ahvardua from the Period 4 defensive ditch.

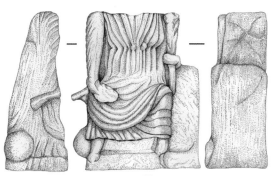

Drawing of the Fortuna statue found close to the Romano-Celtic temple (SF-6772). (M. Hoyle)

16. Priapus statue (SF-10497)
Vindolanda Period 7 (*c.* CE 213–275)
Found lying on a flagged surface inside Stone Fort 2
Height: 425mm; Width: 180mm; Depth: 105mm

The function of religion in the Roman world had different facets and, in many ways, looks very different from organised religion today. The daily interactions people had with many and varied deities meant that religion was ever present, but also that there was a certain degree of freedom to pick and choose one's associations. Deities such as Priapus were meant to invoke fertility, protection, and general good fortune. Priapus is identified by his ithyphallic pose, meaning his erect penis was always a prominent feature of the composition, whether in sculpture or wall painting. He was sometimes invoked as a protector of merchant sailors and is also connected to the fertility of the earth through agriculture and livestock. The statue from Vindolanda is one of only a few Priapic representations in Roman Britain and includes one of the common themes of his good fortune – he holds a full money bag in one hand to show the abundance he may bring. We find similar small objects hoping to invoke fecundity and good fortune at Vindolanda. Small pendants with an erect penis are a regular discovery, as well as phalluses made from almost any material, including wood and stone. A phallus carved from wood found in 1992 may have served such a purpose (W-1992-1062), but could also have been used as a sex toy, and the two purposes need not be mutually exclusive. Priapus was not worshipped in a formal temple space but could be found prominently

Priapus statue with volunteer excavator Liz Pounds after its discovery.

Above left: The Priapus statue.

Above right: Wall painting of Priapus weighing his erect penis, from the House of the Vettii at Pompeii. (Elizabeth M. Greene)

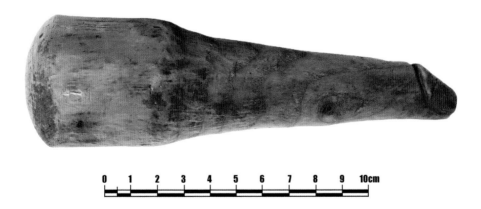

Wooden phallus from a fort ditch (W-1992-1062).

displayed in gardens and anywhere that one might hope to invoke good fortune and fertility. A good example is the fresco of Priapus from the House of the Vettii in Pompeii, in which the god weighs his large penis on a scale to demonstrate its heft. His presence could also help avert the evil eye and ward off the bad spirits that inhabit a space.

17. Evil eye bead (SF-5109)
Vindolanda Periods 7–8 (*c.* third–fourth century CE)
Found during the excavation of the eastern fort wall
Diameter: 14mm

Religion and superstition, which were different concepts in the Roman world, were also present in small, everyday objects that may not at first appear connected to religious belief. For instance, the evil eye could be averted by possessing small objects that hoped to offer protection to their owner. Glass beads with eyes were common talismans not only in the Roman period but may have originated as long ago as the Palaeolithic period. The beads were used to protect the wearer from anyone who might curse an unprotected individual. There are many different production methods but the two examples from Vindolanda were manufactured by dropping different colours of hot glass onto a bead. The first example, found within the third- to fourth-century fort, has a yellow background with eyes that were built up with dots of black, white, and blue glass. The second bead has a blue background with white and blue dots representing the eyes (SF-830). Other objects from Vindolanda also look to ward off the evil eye. The two stones shown here depict faces with a component of the evil eye included. The first one is highly stylised and uses a mini altar to represent the nose (SF-776). The second stone shows the face of a man with a Celtic pointed cap and an eye carved in the space below the figure (SF-518).

Above left: Yellow evil eye bead with blue eyes.

Above middle: Stone depicting a figure wearing a Celtic cap with a disembodied evil eye below (SF-518).

Above right: Portable stone altar with stylised figure and the nose depicted as a small altar (SF-776).

18. Jet votive foot (SF-17340)
Vindolanda Period 9A (*c.* CE 400–600)
Found in a post-Roman fill on the *intervallum* road inside the fort near the *praetorium*
Length: 19mm; Width: 12mm; Depth: 7mm

A primary way for individuals to express their religiosity in antiquity was through votive offerings made to specific deities. This tiny jet foot, no more than 2cm in height, was probably just such an offering. It has a hole drilled through the shin, probably for hanging on a string at one point, and was made with only four toes. It has been interpreted as an ex-voto, or an artefact which was given as an offering to fulfill a vow. Small ex-voto body parts are not unusual on healing sites in Roman Britain, including Bath in Somerset and the temple precinct at Springhead in Kent. Many votives were made from copper-alloy and could have been parts removed from statuettes. The Vindolanda foot is made of jet, which is unusual, but the inclusion of only four toes indicates it may have functioned as a healing votive, perhaps after the loss of a toe.

Small votive objects were common in Roman religion and could include ex-voto offerings, small portable altars, figurines relating to gods or their symbols, and miniature weapons and tools. Two copper-alloy miniature bows (SF-17189 and SF-21100) were found at Vindolanda dating to the late fourth century. Vindolanda has also produced a small copper-alloy mason's pick (SF-15333), uncovered in the 2010 excavations. There is some debate about the meaning of these votive objects. Could they represent the occupation of the dedicant, or could they also just be children's toys? Some of these objects are found as grave goods, others as votive gifts found in religious contexts, while others were probably amuletic pendants. Given the discovery locations of the Vindolanda examples discussed here, it is hard to add any clarity to this question, but there is little doubt that they must have been meaningful to their owners at one point.

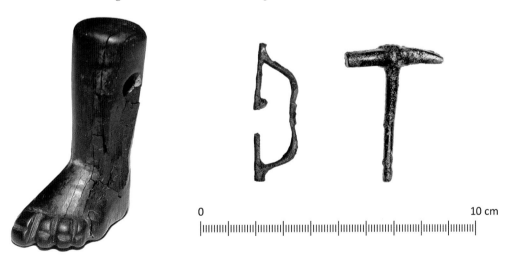

0   10 cm
|ıııııııı|ıııııııı|ıııııııı|ıııııııı|ıııııııı|ıııııııı|ıııııııı|ıııııııı|ıııııııı|ıııııııı|

Above left: Small jet foot probably used as a votive.

Above right: Copper-alloy miniature votive pick (SF-15333) and bow (SF-17189).

19. Portable Christian 'altar' (SF-7539)
Vindolanda Post-Roman levels (*c.* CE 600 +)
Found associated with a sub-Roman structure outside the south-west corner of
Stone Fort 2
Width: 110mm; Height: 82mm; Depth: 22mm

Vindolanda has produced many objects which speak to the changing religious climate of
the late Roman period. The emergence of Christianity is visible in the slow shift in material
culture practices on-site. Objects like this small stone, dating to the sixth century, show an
early form of the Christian chi-rho symbol. It is composed of two Greek letters, chi (X) and
rho (P), the first two letters of the Greek word *christos*, meaning Christ. This stone has been
worn smooth by constant handling, perhaps indicating it was passed among congregants
during religious services or was just well handled by its owner.

Other personal objects like the Christian strap-end shown opposite (SF-17286) were made
of copper-alloy. This strap-end features a priestly figure complete with shepherd's crook
and halo. At the top there is an abstract depiction of a tree of life made from repeating
semicircular impressions. This sort of design is a common late Roman motif and similar
Christian strap-ends featuring peacocks and the tree of life have been found in southern
Britain. This is the most northerly Christian depiction to have been found on a nail cleaning
strap-end from Britain. Other Christian objects from the site include painted Crambeck
pottery and a lead vessel (SF-22145) with carved Christian symbols including fish, boats,
and doves. The tombstone to Brigomaglos (*RIB* 1722A) may reveal to us an individual living
on-site in this post-Roman period when Christianity was on the rise in Britain.

0   10 cm
|⁣||||||||⁣|||||||||⁣|||||||||⁣|||||||||⁣|||||||||⁣|||||||||⁣|||||||||⁣|||||||||⁣|||||||||⁣||||||||⁣|

Portable Christian
object with a
stylised chi-rho
symbol carved onto
the surface.

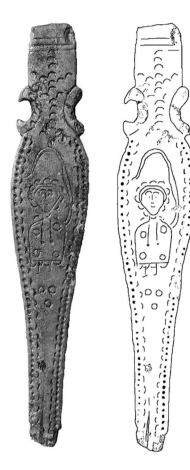

Above: Tombstone of Brigomaglos (*RIB* 1722A).

Right: Copper-alloy strap-end depicting a bishop with his crook and halo (SF-17286).

Below: Drawing of fragments of a lead vessel with Christian symbols etched on the surface (SF-22145).

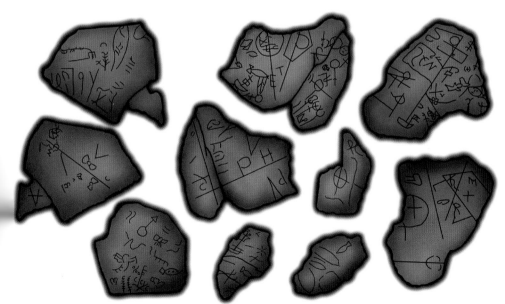

Chapter 4
Dress, Adornment, and the Body

Dress and adornment in the Roman world have seen a great deal of recent study in regional and empire-wide contexts. The way people presented themselves, the objects they displayed prominently, and what they chose to represent their outward expression may offer visual clues to their social status and associations. These clues were especially important within the mixed population of an auxiliary military settlement, where status and social standing were important and the desire to advertise these aspects of one's identity may have been strong. At Vindolanda, small objects of adornment are found daily during the excavation season and a great deal of the collection falls into this category. We often think immediately of small objects like jewellery and brooches, which can be spectacular objects of impeccable craftsmanship, but Vindolanda also produces organic objects that were part of daily personal expression. Textiles and leather objects give us a brief glimpse into the world of decorated items, while wooden objects help us understand the implements used to achieve one's desired appearance.

The expression of a military identity was surely desired by part of the site's population, considering the power and status of the Roman army. This could be accomplished in several ways, even when not clothed in full military attire. Military belts and other regalia would have been easily recognisable as the kit of a soldier and these physical attributes could work to their advantage. Advertisement of status could be achieved through footwear, clothing, and accessories. The range of footwear that was available at Vindolanda is impressive and includes everything from simple handmade shoes to elaborate boots with intricate and detailed cut-out patterning that could reveal a bright splash of colour beneath. From the smallest decorative objects to mundane pieces of clothing, personal adornments reveal something about the individuals who wore them nearly 2,000 years ago.

Above left: Artistic impression of a Roman woman. (M. Hoyle)

Above right: Artistic impression of a Roman soldier. (M. Hoyle)

20. Striped and decorated leather (L-2007-14-B)
Vindolanda Period 3 (*c.* CE 100–105)
Found in organic floor levels of a Period 3 fort structure
Length: 485mm; Width: 205mm; Depth: 1–2mm

The leather objects from Vindolanda are some of the most important means of seeing developing trends in adornment. Typically, shoes are the best-preserved organic objects because of their robust layers of thick leather. Many examples are decorated with stamps of rosettes, eagles, and wheat sheaves (L–2001-49). A few large fragments of sheet leather like this one survive intact enough to reveal that patterns were also applied to the surface of leather. These fragments do not reveal exactly what they were originally a part of, but the application of a burnishing tool that creates a pattern of stripes and criss-crosses is intriguing. We might imagine this technique provided a relatively easy way to decorate the surface of any piece of leather clothing or tentage to create a more decorative finished product. In any sphere of adornment, it seems that decorative and intricate objects demonstrated status and the ability to obtain expensive items. This criss-cross patterning may have been a fairly simple way to achieve this status-bearing appearance with leather garments. We can also see the striped patterning coming through on some of the fragmentary textiles found on-site (Object 10. Inv. 53), suggesting it was used in more than one medium. The execution of a striped pattern was likely more difficult with textile production, but also created a highly decorative piece of clothing that advertised social standing and perhaps a certain level of wealth.

Above left: Leather panel decorated with a burnished pattern.

Above right: Fragment of striped textile (Object 10.Inv.53).

Left: Leather shoe sole stamped with wheat sheaves (L–2001-49).

21. Aqua glass bead (SF-23543)
Vindolanda Period 6A (*c.* CE 160–200)
Found on the top of the rampart mound inside Stone Fort 1
Diameter: 31.4mm; Perforation diameter: 11.1mm

Glass beads are not unusual finds but this unique large glass bead with aqua and yellow waves is unparalleled in the collection. Whether it was used as a strung piece of jewellery or as some other decorative flourish is unknown, but it would have been a stunning addition to anyone's personal appearance. Researchers suggest that beads were used as adornment for horse tack, weapon sheaths, and even *dolabra* (entrenching tools), in addition to their better-known use in necklaces and earrings.

Glass beads from Vindolanda come in a variety of shapes and colours, including a blue heart-shaped bead and multicoloured wave beads. The most common beads are blue and green glass beads, favoured as cheaper imitations of emeralds and sapphires. The only examples that survive on their string are two glass beads (one green-glass style and the other red-blue-white) that were strung on a copper-alloy wire (SF-7674). The variation between these two beads makes us wonder how the whole object appeared. Was this a repeating pattern or could it have been a string of random beads? There are a number of personal objects made of glass found within the collection, including bracelets and finger rings. Most glass bangles are fragmentary but there is one complete example from Vindolanda that reveals the full form of these striking objects (SF-5930).

0   10 cm

Above left: Large aqua glass bead just after discovery in 2022.

Above right: Complete aqua glass bracelet (SF-5930).

Below: Two glass beads on a copper-alloy wire (SF-7674).

22. 'Medusa' finger ring (SF-18)
Vindolanda Period 6B (*c.* CE 200–212)
Found in the commanding officer's residence of the Severan-period fort
Outer diameter: 23mm; Inner diameter: 20mm; Depth: 8mm

The 'Medusa' finger ring is a good example of the high-quality objects that made their way to this frontier fort. It is one of only a handful of gold objects from Vindolanda and its value suggests that it belonged to an elite individual who could afford such luxury. Finger rings in the Roman world were very much a part of one's personal adornment and signified status and belonging. In fact, Roman law governed who could wear rings of various metals, reserving gold for only the highest-ranking members of society, while iron rings could be worn by a broader sector of the population. The cameo placed into the bezel of this ring, though somewhat worn now, depicts the face of Medusa and may have doubled as a sort of protective amulet. The shoulders of the ring are wide and decorated with incised lines forming a radiating pattern from the bezel down to the band of the ring. The object is rather heavy and must have made quite a statement for its wearer. A few other rings found on-site, such as the gold ring with a wide, flat bezel (SF-127) and the *'anima mea'* gold ring with carnelian stone (SF-300, see Object 43), suggest their owners enjoyed high status, or perhaps splashed out on an expensive item. These rings were also found in third-century occupation contexts, indicating that some very high-quality jewellery found its way to site at this time.

Left: Gold ring with Medusa cameo.

Below: Gold ring with flat bezel (SF-127).

Roman brooches take many different forms, from the simple to the extraordinary, and the Vindolanda collection has hundreds of examples. In the Roman world brooches were used to hold clothes onto the body, and an individual might wear several at one time depending on the needs of the clothing. Some brooches were simple, not much more than a modern safety pin, but others could show the wealth of the wearer or even symbolise cultural or religious affiliations.

Dragonesque brooches like this one are one of many forms of zoomorphic plate brooches and have been interpreted as a Romano-British design, since they are found almost exclusively in Roman Britain and show Celtic influences. The Vindolanda dragonesque brooch is intricately enamelled, like many examples of this type. It has an S-shaped body with animal heads, complete with upstanding ears and curled snouts at both ends. The pin is attached around the neck of the upper head and is hooked over the lower neck. Another example follows a similar pattern and is adorned with equally ornate style (SF-8928). In general, this brooch type dates to the first century CE.

The Vindolanda collection also holds artefacts which reflect the diverse origins of the troops who were stationed at the site. One such object is this military brooch (SF-9570) that was found in contexts contemporary with the occupation of the Ninth Cohort of Batavians at Vindolanda in a style originating from Batavia (modern Netherlands). One of hundreds of brooches in the collection, the trumpet brooch shown here (SF-23405) also reveals the range of styles available on-site.

Two dragonesque brooches
from Vindolanda (SF-8928 and
SF-4659).

41

Batavian-style brooch made of copper-alloy (SF-9570).

Trumpet brooch from the anaerobic layers of the site (SF-23405).

24. Hair-moss wig (SF-3542)
Vindolanda Periods 3–4 (*c.* CE 100–120)
Found in the floor levels of a timber structure inside the fort
Cap width: 170mm; Strand length: 280mm

Ancient authors and sculptures of elite women found throughout the empire make it clear that the Romans used hair wigs. Experimental archaeology has tested the amount of added hair that was required to execute some of the elaborate styles worn by empresses and other elite women, but no actual wigs that help to better understand this elaborate tradition have ever been found. At Vindolanda, however, an extraordinary object was found in 1986 that gives us some idea of how regular people may have worn a hairpiece. The object is made from common hair moss (*polytrichum commune*), a plant that is found throughout the local area around Vindolanda (compare to Object 6, the hair-moss helmet crest). The object was examined by J. P. Wild, who determined the construction type is fairly complex, using bundles of hair-moss stems knotted into a cone at the apex and plaiting around the bundles to form the tightly woven cap. Loose strands were then left to fall from the woven cap for *c.* 20–25 cm on the sides and back, and roughly 7–10 cm at the front, like a fringe. A similar object was recovered at the beginning of the twentieth century from the late-Flavian levels in the Roman fort at Newstead. Both caps have been variously identified as unfinished baskets, but it seems now that this is an untenable identification. The Vindolanda object has all the hallmarks of a wig or some sort of headgear, including a tightly woven cap over the top of the head and strands that fall loose on two sides and at the back, leaving the area of the face open.

Wig or hairpiece made
from hair moss.

25. Comb with leather case (W-669 and L-1989-2659)
Vindolanda Period 2 (c. CE 90–100)
Found in a room of the commanding officer's residence
Width: 73.32mm; Height: 49.38mm; Depth: 7.62mm

This wooden comb, complete with its leather carrying case, is a beautiful example of its object type. Both the fine and coarse teeth are expertly carved up to the guidelines that run along the central bar. There is just the faintest hint of a maker's mark left along the centre showing that the manufacturer wanted to advertise their craftsmanship. Only a small number of these imported utilitarian objects have been stamped by their makers.

The Vindolanda collection has over 160 of these small, imported combs. All made of boxwood, these delicately carved objects had a very important role to play in nit management and were also used to style hair. Owning your own comb and being sure you could identify it was probably important, and many of the combs from the collection show different designs, modifications, and personalisation. Owners scratched their own design or message into the wood, as shown on the example owned by Carantus (W-2002-39A). He added a graffito onto his comb reading: 'CARANTVS APICTINVS'. Carantus was presumably the owner of the comb and hoped not to lose this common yet personally valuable object. The most highly decorated comb in the collection has fretted terminals and a metal plate with a figure of a soldier adorning the central bar (W-2010-17B), indicating that these objects were not entirely utilitarian.

0   10 cm
|ıllıllıl|ıllıllıl|ıllıllıl|ıllıllıl|ıllıllıl|ıllıllıl|ıllıllıl|ıllıllıl|ıllıllıl|ıllıllıl|

Boxwood hair comb with leather carrying case.

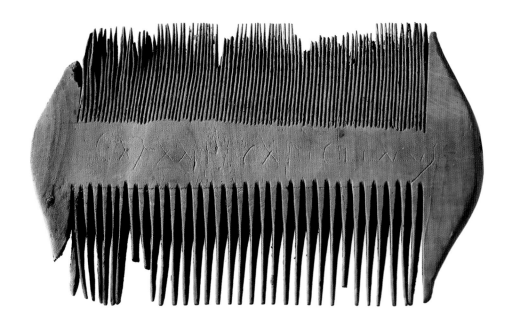

Wooden hair comb with a graffito reading 'CARANTVS APICTINVS' (W-2002-39A).

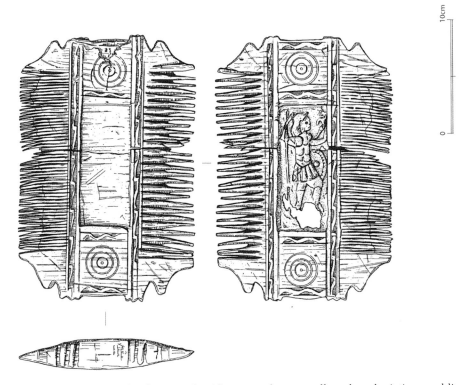

Beautifully carved wooden hair comb with a central copper-alloy plate depicting a soldier (W-2010-17B). (M. Hoyle)

Chapter 5
Economy, Trade, and Industry on the Frontier

The economy and industry of a Roman fort can be investigated in many different ways and the evidence found at Vindolanda has helped to provide new perspectives for understanding the daily operations of a military settlement. The Roman army had an enormous impact on the landscape and economy of the territory it occupied, both by creating opportunity through supply to the troops and new settlements, and by disrupting existing networks. Exactly how the economy operated in each province and frontier zone is still under investigation and one single economic model is unlikely to pertain to all Roman frontiers.

At Vindolanda we can investigate a localised response to shifting economic practices including trade, industry, and manufacturing. The archaeology allows investigation of the goods coming in and out of the fort but also the spaces of trade and industry that were part of the daily grind of economic activity. The writing tablets tell us about the specific goods that were coming into the fort, such as hides and foodstuffs, but also about the daily work operations of the soldiers, such as what structures they were building and where they were assigned for manufacturing. The preservation of wood and leather alongside the standard objects such as coins, pottery, and metal tools at Vindolanda offer an exceptionally detailed picture of the process of manufacturing and give us a robust understanding of this aspect of life in a military settlement.

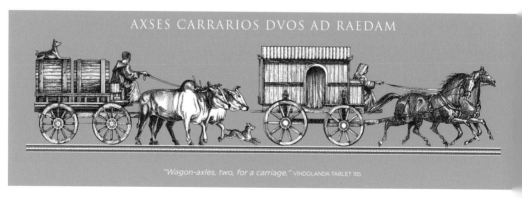

AXSES CARRARIOS DVOS AD RAEDAM

"Wagon-axles, two, for a carriage." VINDOLANDA TABLET 185

Artistic impression of two Roman wagon types. (Peter Phillips)

Vindolanda's main road through the *vicus* towards the west gate.

26. Gold coin of Nero (C-2612)
Reign of Nero (CE 54–68)
Found in the construction material of a fourth-century rampart inside the fort
Diameter: 18.56mm; Depth: 2.17mm

Discussion of the Roman economy often conjures thoughts of high-value coins and trade. The soldiers at Vindolanda were paid primarily with bronze and silver coins (*sestertii* and *denarii*) through the second and third centuries, resulting in an abundance of those coins found during excavations. The site has produced only a single gold coin (*aureus*), and the location of its discovery allows us to appreciate the long lives of some Roman coins. It was minted under Emperor Nero (CE 54–68) but was very worn and found in a fourth-century archaeological context inside the fort. The coin would not have been legal tender after the coinage reforms enacted under Constantine in the early fourth century, which introduced new forms of gold and silver coinage. Perhaps this helps explain why it was discarded in the fourth century, but the metal itself would continue to hold intrinsic value, so it may also represent an accidental loss. How it remained in circulation for so long is also a mystery, but gold in any form was surely a valued commodity. It may also have been kept by its owner as a talisman of sorts, but we are unable to reconstruct the itinerary of this object over its centuries-long life. This single gold coin is an excellent reminder that objects may have been kept for quite some time before deposition in the archaeological record.

Gold coin of Nero.

27. Duty roster writing tablet (*Tab. Vindol.* 155)
Vindolanda Period 3 (*c.* CE 100–105)
Found in a structure inside the fort
Dimensions: varied fragments

The daily tasks of production and manufacture needed to keep a military fort operational are on display clearly in the writing tablet shown here, which includes a list of jobs and the number of men assigned to each. The text is only partially preserved but the surviving list of activities taking place on the site is still impressive:

25 April, in the workshops, 343 men.
of these: shoemakers, 12
builders to the bath-house, 18
for lead ...
for ... wagons (?) ...
... hospital ...
to the kilns ...
for clay ...
plasterers ...
for ... tents (?) ...
for rubble ...

Soldiers were assigned to various building projects such as construction of a bathhouse, extraction of raw materials like clay, and work in active manufacturing spaces like the kilns. It is clear from this tablet that the work was done locally and that we are likely to find the corresponding work areas at Vindolanda at some point, if we have not already. In the excavations of the North Field at Vindolanda an industrial area was uncovered that included the two kilns seen in the image here, as well as evidence of brick and tile production at one point. Vindolanda also produces a large number of tools, such as large agricultural implements like pickaxes, spades and hoes, alongside small items like knives, tongs, trowels and small picks (SF-23897), which combine to show a range of manufacturing activities.

Ink-on-wood writing tablet recording a duty roster.

Above: Excavations of a brick and tile kiln in Vindolanda's North Field.

Left: Small pickaxe with wooden handle in situ during excavation in 2023.

28. Clay mould for bust figurine (SF-18689)
Late first to early second century CE
Found in the fill of a large kiln in the North Field
Height: 91mm; Width: 69mm; Depth: 43mm

The tablet above references workers assigned to the kilns at Vindolanda and these just may be the same kilns found in the industrial complex in the North Field in 2014. A large stone kiln that showed very little evidence of firing sat alongside a smaller kiln and a firepit that saw extensive use in the late first and second centuries. One of the most unique finds to emerge from that space was this oval clay mould used to create a small bust of the god Apollo. Its backside was left rough in its final form, while the front shows extensive detail in the face of the figure. No evidence has yet been found for the finished product, but the mould may have produced small busts similar to the one of Apollo shown here (SF-20534), but in clay rather than bronze. This object certainly demonstrates the talent of its creator and suggests that Vindolanda may have produced some fine products for the region.

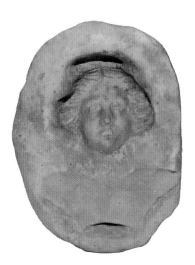

Right: Clay mould of Apollo from the North Field kiln.

Below: Drawing of a copper-alloy bust of Apollo.
(M. Hoyle)

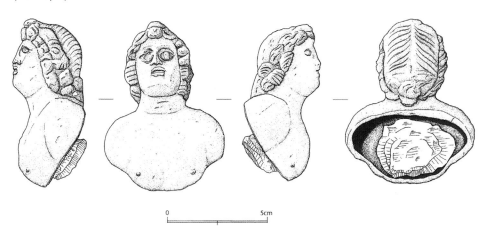

29. The workbench of 'ATTO' (W-1994-1304)
Vindolanda Period 4 (*c.* CE 105–120)
Found on a floor surface in a fort structure
Length: 938mm; Width: 172mm; Depth: 36.7mm

This extraordinary object offers a glimpse into the people who kept a military fort operational through manufacturing and industry. What at first appears to be a mundane wooden plank reveals itself as the workbench of an individual named Atto, who carved his name into its surface. It may have been later reused in the floor or discarded before the structure in which it was found was buried. The identification of the plank as a repurposed workbench is confirmed by the many tool marks that are found on its surface. They are in a random pattern around the central area of the bench, where the name of 'ATTO' was inscribed in capital letters. The tool marks are mostly 10mm wide divots in a half-moon shape that may have come from a leather working tool. One can imagine Atto at work on the bench, straddling it with legs on either side, and pressing the tool into the surface of a leather object. It would strike through the leather and leave an impression in the soft wood supporting the object underneath. Many leather objects in the collection, from shoe uppers to horse chamfrons, have decorative elements that are made by a punch like this one. Punch marks in the shape of an 's', half-moons, tear-drop shapes, and simple straight lines that form a pattern are all found on leather items at Vindolanda. The site also produces complete examples of punch tools, the most basic of which are awls, which sometimes have decorative handles (SF-23863). These unique objects reveal something of the process of manufacturing, while also providing a rare image of an individual at work in the ancient world.

Complete wooden worktop inscribed with the name ATTO.

Detail of Atto's worktop showing the inscribed name and punch marks.

Leatherworking awl found in June 2023.

One of the extraordinary finds from the Vindolanda wood collection is part of a wagon wheel with many of its components intact. Several wheel spokes and other vehicle parts discarded into ditches or reused for other purposes are also found in the collection. Wheels remind us of the many commercial endeavours that took place around the fort and give us a good sense of the hive of activity that once surrounded military forts and settlements in antiquity. These commercial activities are on display also in the Vindolanda writing tablets with discussion of cart loads of goods coming into the fort and inventory lists of the storehouses showing just how many commodities must have travelled to the settlement every week. In one of the most complete letters in the corpus of Vindolanda tablets, written by Octavius to Candidus (*Tab. Vindol.* 343), we are shown the large-scale operation of supplying a military fort. The letter discusses huge amounts of grain (5,000 *modii*), hundreds of leather hides from nearby Catterick, sinew, and *braces* (a type of cereal for beer making) among its commodities. The operation of supplying a military fort is enormous and we are reminded of these mundane yet critical activities by the presence of everyday finds such as a wooden wheel.

Wagon wheel in situ during discovery and excavation.

Wagon wheel on display in Vindolanda's museum.

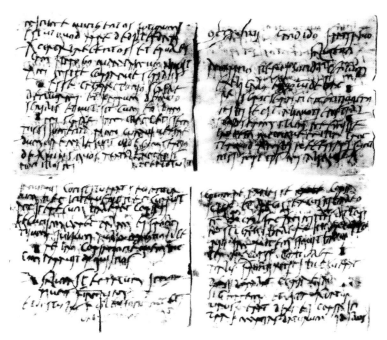

Letter from Octavius to Candidus (*Tab. Vindol.* 343).

31. Complete tent panels (L-2001-255-a, Panels 1–8)
Vindolanda Period 1 (*c.* CE 85–90)
Found in the fill of a defensive fort ditch
Length: 590–610mm; Width: 420–498mm; Depth: 1–3mm

The leather assemblage at Vindolanda allows us to reconstruct something of the economy of the fort, particularly the goods that were shipped into the fort from elsewhere. Huge amounts of leather in the form of hides entered the settlement on a regular basis and we find the finished products in the form of tent panels, shoes, and smaller leather objects in almost every context that preserves organic remains. The letter from Octavius to Candidus (*Tab. Vindol.* 343, pictured on the previous page) reveals some of the intensity and cost surrounding the movement of hides and leather items around the northern frontier, suggesting they were a very important commodity in the economy of goods moving in and out of the fort.

The object seen here is one of eight panels of the same tent found together in a fort ditch during the 2001 excavations. These are in pristine condition and it is possible to reconstruct the seams that attached different panels. The leather strips that support the seams were even intact upon discovery. The Vindolanda leather assemblage has allowed Carol van Driel-Murray to complete a full reconstruction of a Roman tent, pictured below, using another hoard of leather found in the 1980s (L-1987-1016). This group of panels fortuitously included key corner and edge pieces, allowing researchers to reconstruct the height and structure of a Roman tent. This information is used by reenactment groups such as the Ermine Street Guard to display accurate replicas of military equipment like the tents pictured opposite.

One of the eight tent panels found together in 2001.

Right: Reconstruction drawing of a Roman tent based on Vindolanda evidence. (C. van Driel-Murray)

Below: Ermine Street Guard replica tents on-site at Vindolanda.

This collection of *terra sigillata* (Samian Ware) was found discarded into a ditch still stacked together. The small notches and broken rims on almost all vessels suggest that the shipment had been damaged during transport and subsequently tossed away upon arrival at Vindolanda. Its date in the late CE 80s is supported by comparison to vessel forms and decoration in an unopened crate of *terra sigillata* found at Pompeii (destroyed in CE 79), and the lack of *sigillata* forms that are found in the earlier Flavian-period sites in Scotland. This tableware was made in La Graufesenque, a major production site in southern Gaul (modern France) and was produced in great quantities as a cheaper alternative to metal wares and glass vessels. The assemblage from the ditch is not a complete dinner service, as it lacks most of the small drinking cups that should have been included and perhaps survived their journey intact, but it is typical of some of the best quality pottery of the late first century in northern Britain.

The vessels were found together with a complete glass bottle and the contents of a barrel of oysters which were also discarded into the ditch with the pottery. Even on the frontier, the Romans had access to both basic and more exotic supplies, although apparently their quality could not always be guaranteed. Samian vessels are found ubiquitously during the excavations, but they also had enough value that we often find lead repairs to broken pots. Also common are objects made from broken and disused Samian Ware, such as gaming counters and spindle whorls.

Above left: Samian hoard found discarded in the Period 1 ditch on display at Vindolanda.

Above right: Sherd of Samian ware bowl from recent excavations with maker's mark.

33. Box lid with triskelion (SF-22766)
Vindolanda Period 9A (*c.* CE 400–600)
Found above the floor surface of a stone cavalry barrack in the fort
Length: 147mm; Width: 120mm; Depth: 12mm

Another exceptional object exemplifies the role of trade from further afield in the late Roman period. The box lid with a triskelion decoration on the top is made of copper-alloy and is mounted onto an iron sheet to offer support. It is very fragile but the central triskelion decoration, with raised border edges and three concave cobalt blue-glass circles, is unlike anything else in the collection. The decorated copper-alloy upper plate has been carefully embossed with great skill and then folded over the underlying iron support sheet. There are no signs of hinges indicating that the lid simply sat on top of the box sides and base.

The triskelion is a design with rotational symmetry, which will look the same as it is rotated. Its form dates back to the Neolithic period but is seen through the Roman period and is used still today. It became favoured by Celtic metalworkers because of its association with their belief that the number three was auspicious. This object may be of Celtic-Irish origin and, given its date, could demonstrate the emerging new triskelion trinity symbolism of the Father, Son, and Holy Ghost. Whatever the meaning, this was a high-status object, expertly produced and beautiful in its simplicity of design. The iron support plate has been instrumental in ensuring that the lid survived until the present day.

Copper-alloy box lid with triskelion design.

The extraordinary objects discussed here, especially in the context of trade of quality goods, also conjure the need for security on-site. Security is not just a modern problem and those living at Vindolanda must have dealt with theft and petty pilfering. People took steps to protect their belongings by marking objects with their name or individualised mark. For additional security, locks on boxes and doors were a sensible precaution when available. This object is a wooden locking mechanism, a survivor of the oldest form of locking apparatus, generally known as an Egyptian lock. It is one of two similar wooden locks from the site. The Egyptian system used internal tumblers which were raised by special wood or bone lift keys like the one pictured here (W-1988-582).

Vindolanda has also produced copper-alloy and iron keys, as well as lock pins and plates. There are even some small keys attached to rings and worn on fingers for smaller boxes and a form of padlock. Although the Romans made huge advancements in locking systems by introducing metal locks, a determined thief could still conquer their systems. The Vindolanda writing tablets illuminate the challenges of locking away precious articles. Julius Verecundus, the Commanding Officer of the First Cohort of Tungrians based at Vindolanda in CE 85–90, writes to his slave Audax (in *Tab. Vindol.* 890) that 'you have sent another key with the box than you should have done, for this is said to be (the key) of the little storeroom'.

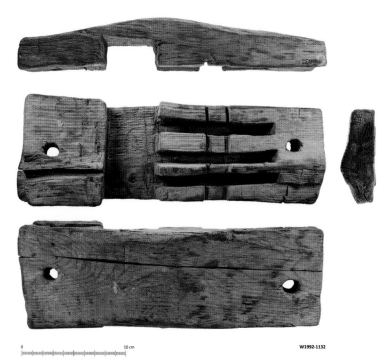

0   10 cm   W1992-1132

Wooden locking mechanism.
(R. Sands)

60

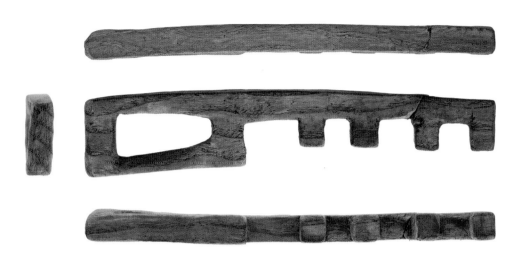

Wooden key with teeth (W-1988-582). (R. Sands)

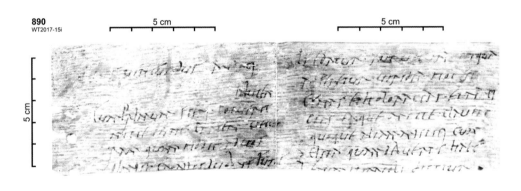

Ink-on-wood writing tablet recording letter from Julius Verecundus to his slave Audax (*Tab. Vindol.* 890).

61

Chapter 6
Recreation and Leisure

Leisure time must have been a key component of life in a military settlement and the archaeology in and around forts suggests there was plenty to keep the soldiers busy outside their official duties. We can imagine the bathhouses, one of which existed at almost every Roman fort and settlement in the empire, provided much of the daily relaxation after intense periods of activity. At Vindolanda a bathhouse from the pre-Hadrianic phases (*c.* CE 85–120) was located to the south of the fort and in the third century there was a large

Aerial view of Vindolanda's third-/fourth-century bathhouse. (Photographer: Aerial-Cam)

Reconstruction drawing of the third-/fourth-century bathhouse.

bathhouse located in the extramural settlement to the west of the fort walls. Bathhouses were not only for washing but also served as locations for gaming and social gatherings, and in some larger structures, like the imperial baths in Rome, it seems there were libraries, food stalls, and a whole range of leisure pursuits. The image of the Vindolanda bathhouse above shows the structures surrounding a bathhouse, such as shops and taverns for drinking and socialising.

Gaming was certainly popular in the Roman world and the most common games seem to be those that used a gridded game board and small rounded gaming pieces. Portable game boards are found scratched into tiles and stones, but they could also be found inscribed permanently in the surfaces of public spaces, such as one found in the Forum in Rome itself, located on the steps of the Basilica Julia. Vindolanda has produced a number of game boards and thousands of small gaming counters, indicating board games were a very popular way to pass the time out on the frontier.

Only a few toilet seats have been found anywhere in the Roman empire and wooden examples are especially rare. The seat found at Vindolanda is exceptional evidence of the mechanisms of toilets and similar facilities in Roman military settlements. Toilet blocks were located either on their own or as part of a larger structure. On military sites they are often found in the corners of the fort, ideally in locations where the effluent would flow downhill and downwind. In larger Roman settlements, public toilets were located in the centre of towns and cities next to houses or shops and were part of the fabric of urban life. Toilets were also very commonly part of public bathhouses and both complexes at Vindolanda incorporated this feature. Bathhouses were generally a key location for cleaning and caring for the body, as well as a site of leisure activities. Dozens of gaming counters have been found in both stand-alone toilet blocks and those within bathhouses, indicating that leisure activities took place even within the toilet areas. The site has also produced several bath clogs (*sculponae*), which were specially designed wooden shoes with thick platforms on the bottom to raise the wearer above the moisture and heat of the bathhouse floor (W-1986-136). One can imagine that these would also be useful when visiting the public toilet block while enjoying the baths.

Wooden toilet seat soon after discovery.

Above: Toilet block in the south-eastern corner of the stone fort at Vindolanda.

Right: Wooden bath clog (W-1986-136). (R. Sands)

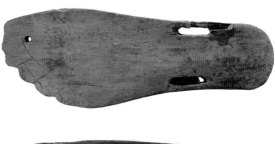

W1986-0136

36. Stone gaming board (SF-21894)
Vindolanda Period 7 (*c.* CE 213–275)
Found in a 'strip house' in the extramural settlement
Length: 320mm; Width: 200mm; Depth: 28mm

Many of the board games that we play today, including backgammon and Nine Men's Morris, have a tradition which started in ancient times. Research has found that *Ludus Latrunculorum* (the game of brigands or soldiers) was the most popular game in Roman Britain. Similar to draughts, this strategy game required two players, a board with incised squares, and gaming counters. The objective was to 'capture' the opponent's pieces by trapping them between two of your own. We can look to ancient literary sources, including the poetry of Ovid and Martial, to give some indication of the rules of the game but, unfortunately, the full instructions are unknown.

To date this is the only type of board game found at Vindolanda. Sixteen stone or ceramic boards have been excavated making Vindolanda's collection the largest in Roman Britain. The boards show great diversity in their quality and craftsmanship; some were carefully incised into the stone while others were just rough scratches. The Vindolanda collection holds numerous gaming counters made of different materials including glass, bone, ceramic, and stone. Dice games were also played on-site, and their popularity is indicated by the many bone dice we find on-site (e.g. SF-5918, SF-8767), as well as a finely decorated bone-dice shaker (SF-3714). Dice with lead-weighted plugs have also been found, which altered the probability for certain rolls, presumably in favour of the roller.

Above left: Largest stone gaming board from Vindolanda.

Above right: Bone dice (SF-5918 and SF-8767) and dice shaker (SF-3714).

37. Gladiator glass (SF-711, SF-5454, SF-11080)
Vindolanda Period 7 (*c.* CE 213–275)
Found in parts in a shallow pit inside the tavern in the extramural settlement
and a defensive fort ditch
Length: *c.* 180mm (all shards flattened); Max. height: 50mm

This fine piece of glass is painted with a scene of figures fighting in gladiatorial combat. It was probably made in Cologne (modern Germany), which was a production site of many painted vessels similar to this example. The gladiatorial scene was hand-painted onto the surface of the glass vessel and reveals delicate work on the part of the artist. Recent research by Louisa Campbell on the glass vessel using portable X-Ray fluorescence (pXRF), a non-destructive analytical technique, confirmed the enamelling on the vessel was made of a complex recipe of mixed pigments such as lapis lazuli, hematite, and lead antimonate.

In addition to its stunning quality, this object also has an amazing archaeological story. It appears to have been used in a tavern in the third century and broken in that space. One large piece of the broken cup was buried in a shallow pit in the floor of the tavern and was discovered during excavations in 2007. The rest of the broken cup must have been taken out with the rubbish and discarded in the fort ditch about 20 metres away. During excavations in 1991, a large piece from the vessel had been found in the ditch. When the new piece was discovered in 2007, the relationship was immediately recognised and the two pieces fit together perfectly, completing the leg of one of the running figures. Finally, another small fragment that had been found in 1972 was identified in the collection. This shard, which initially had had no clear join to anything in the collection, fitted perfectly onto the 2007 fragment and completed two more legs of a gladiator. This glass vessel and its archaeological story highlight the importance of ongoing research and excavation.

Above left: Painted glass vessel depicting a gladiatorial scene.

Above right: Shard of glass with a small fish depicted (SF-1268).

38. Tankard staves (W-1993-1218)
Vindolanda Period 6 (*c.* CE 140–160)
Found in the fill of a defensive fort ditch
Height: 120.1mm; Width: 23.1mm; Depth: 12.6mm

Drinking and visiting the tavern would have been an important part of the leisure culture for many of those individuals living at Vindolanda. This is evidenced in the archaeological record by the many vessels that transported and stored beverages, as well as the vessels that were used for drinking. Not all drinking vessels were as exquisite as the gladiator glass, and the majority of finds are more mundane, such as parts of wooden tankards probably used to drink beer (W-1993-1254 also pictured, with tankard bases, W-2005-8-A and W-2005-18-A). Though there is no definite proof of its contents yet, there is a strong connection to beer drinking on-site, seen clearly in the text of some writing tablets. A letter from the *decurion* (cavalry officer) Masculus to the commander of the Batavians, Flavius Cerialis, requests more beer to be sent to his fellow soldiers at the fort (*Tab. Vindol.* 628) in the early second century CE. Other tablets mention the ingredients for beer and references are made to brewers and 'malsters' at the fort in the late first and early second centuries. Evidence suggests that beer drinking was part of the culture among at least the early groups of Tungrians and Batavians at the fort.

Other finds include ring-necked flagons and vessels that stored and held beverages. These are found in some quantity in certain buildings that probably functioned at least in part as taverns. Only a small number of wine amphorae have been found at Vindolanda, but the few present suggest that some wine was drunk on-site. Additionally, a large part of the pottery assemblages from the site includes bowls and cups that no doubt held liquid refreshment used in the social rituals of eating and drinking.

Ring-necked flagon from Vindolanda.

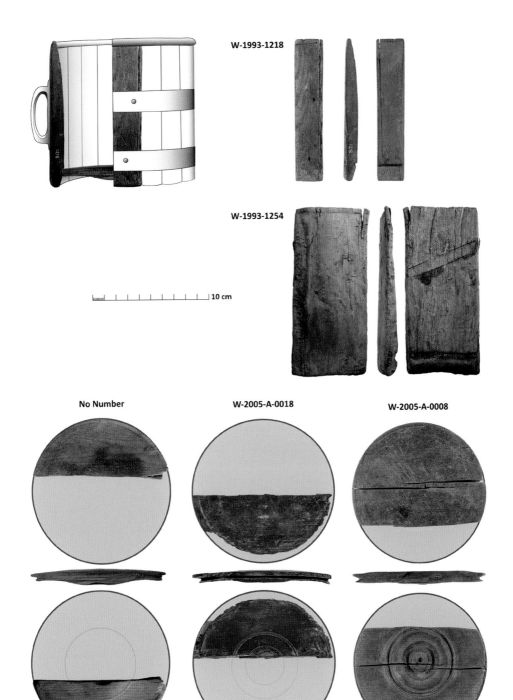

W-1993-1218

W-1993-1254

10 cm

No Number

W-2005-A-0018

W-2005-A-0008

Wooden tankard staves and bases with an illustration of a complete Roman tankard. (R. Sands)

39. Boxing gloves (L-2017-120 and L-2017-149)
Vindolanda Period 4 (c. CE 105–120)
Found in a cavalry barrack inside the fort
Small (L-2017-120): Length: 125mm; Width: 27mm; Depth: 70mm
Large (L-2017-149): Length: 147mm; Width: 100mm; Depth: 43mm

Two pieces of leather of a type not previously discovered at Vindolanda were found during the excavations in 2017. These two unassuming but remarkable objects have been identified as a sparring or practice form of boxing gloves (*caestus*). We can see these depicted on mosaics and sculptures from the Roman period, such as the bronze boxer statue now in the Palazzo Massimo Museum in Rome. Boxing was apparently a popular pastime for Roman soldiers. Both gloves were cut from a single piece of leather and folded into a pouch-like configuration, tapering to leather 'arms' which were slotted into one another, forming an oval shape with an inner hole into which a hand can still be easily inserted.

The pouch of the larger glove was stuffed with shock-absorbing grasses and bracken when it was discovered, while the smaller glove has an insert of hard coiled leather. Both gloves have a flattened lower edge forming a hard ridge of leather designed to cause damage to an opponent. Other evidence for boxing emerged from the excavations in 2004, when the fragments of a silver plate featuring a boxer were discovered in the extramural settlement (SF-9642; 54.5mm × 63.8mm). The fragment features a male figure in a typical boxing position with his fists raised to head-height and his left fist extended in front of his body. He wears his gloves and an almost theatrical mask-type expression of aggression.

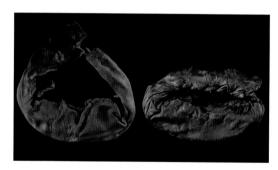
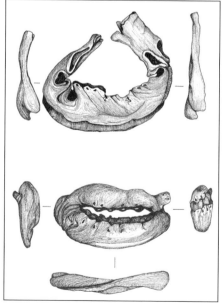

Above and right: Photograph and illustrations of the boxing gloves.

Above: Detail of a bronze statue of a Roman boxer in the Palazzo Massimo Museum in Rome. (Photo: Elizabeth M. Greene)

Right: Fragment of a silver plate depicting a boxer with hands raised (SF-9642).

Chapter 7
The Power of Words and Writing

The power of words in antiquity is vividly displayed at Vindolanda. The corpus of writing tablets, both ink tablets and wax stylus tablets, has offered some of the most evocative images of life on the Roman frontier and has allowed us to see those people who would otherwise be entirely invisible in the archaeological record. The letters between

Reconstructed stone altars from Vindolanda now in the garden at the Vindolanda Museum.

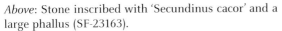

Above: Stone inscribed with 'Secundinus cacor' and a large phallus (SF-23163).

Right: Altar dedicated to Volcanus from the *Vicani Vindolandesses* now in the Vindolanda Museum (*RIB* 1700).

officers' wives hold what may be the first handwriting of a woman in western Europe (*Tab. Vindol.* 291, see Object 7) and may also contain evidence of the education of children and others in the fort (*Tab. Vindol.* 118, see Object 40). Inscriptions on stone reveal the military units in residence and their commanders, the names of those who lived and died on the site, and the deities they worshipped on a daily basis. One can appreciate the variety of stone inscriptions produced in antiquity from the images shown here. Perfect lettering is on display in large dedications placed in the *principia,* the replicas of which are found in the garden at Vindolanda, while the more rustic writing of the altar to Volcanus from the *Vicani Vindolandesses* (inhabitants of the Vindolanda *vicus*; *RIB* 1700) and the Secundinus stone (SF-23163) reveal less-practised execution. Small objects were more personal and show us that people scratched their names on their cups, perhaps hoping to deter theft or loss. Sentimental mementos use words to show love of another or to express various personal sentiments.

The amount of writing found in the Roman world, even on the edge of the empire in Britain, suggests that the concept of writing became important to many people quite quickly. The old image of an almost entirely illiterate provincial population has now been replaced with new and different ideas about literacy, suggesting that more of the population than previously thought had some access to the written word, even if they were not fully literate. Proximity to the Roman army was certainly a factor in the spread of the written word, especially in Latin, but we ought to imagine that this influence could extend far into the surrounding community, with different levels of literacy in different sectors of the population.

40. Ink writing pen (SF-3613)
Vindolanda Period 3 (c. CE 100–105)
Found in the *praetorium* kitchen refuse pit with writing tablets
Iron nib: 15mm wide
Wood shaft: Length: 90mm; Diameter: 12mm

Writing implements are common at Vindolanda. Over the years, archaeologists have found iron ink-pen nibs, including one complete example with its wooden shaft, as well as hundreds of iron and copper-alloy stylus pens. This almost complete ink pen, with its iron spiral nib and wooden shaft, would have been used as a 'dip and scratch' pen. It even has a small hole down the wooden shaft to help with possible capillary action for the ink. This type of ink pen could have been used to write a number of the tablets in the Vindolanda collection, including excerpts from classical texts. The tablet shown here (*Tab. Vindol.* 118), dating to around CE 100, was excavated from the commanding officer's residence and has been interpreted as a writing exercise. It records a quotation from Virgil's *Aeneid* (Book 9, line 473): '*Intera pavidam volitans pinnata p(?) ubem SEG.*' The sentence was written mostly correctly, but after *pinnata* the writer should have followed with *per urbem* and someone else has added the letters *SEG*, probably short for *segniter* or 'sloppy work'. Who was practising their writing and could it have been one of the prefect's children? We will probably never know, but this tablet helps to show that education in writing was important in this household. At least another four fragments of writing from classical Latin texts exist at Vindolanda and there are hopes to find more with continuing excavations. The Romans also used wax stylus tablets that were more robust and have a recessed face that was filled with wax. Metal stylus pens, some of which were very detailed and beautiful objects, were used to scratch the message into the surface of the wax (SF-4107).

Ink pen with iron nib and a wooden shaft.

Above: Ink-on-wood writing tablet recording a child's writing lesson (*Tab. Vindol.* 118).

Right: Wax stylus tablet immediately after discovery in the field.

Below: Highly decorated stylus pen made from different metals (SF-4107).

10 cm

41. Tombstone of Titus Annius (*RIB* 3364)
Stone originally dates to *c.* CE 120
Found reused in a fourth-century context in the *praetorium* of Stone Fort 2
Height: 60cm; Width: 50cm; Depth: 18cm

In the Roman world inscriptions on stone were commonly used to commemorate the dead. This tombstone commemorated Titus Annius of the First Cohort of Tungrians. It was created sometime around CE 117 when violence erupted in the region, but was found reused in the fabric of the *praetorium* during a fourth-century phase of the building. The inscription records Titus Annius' death *in bello,* or 'in the war', which may refer to these events that took place in the region recorded in Latin literary sources. Tombstones rely upon the written word to preserve the memory of individuals and often include sentimental words like 'most dear' or 'sweetest' to describe the deceased. Only about one quarter of this inscription survives, but we learn a few personal details: we know Titus Annius was a centurion and that he had a son. There are a number of Latin inscriptions from Vindolanda recording dedications to deities, among other things, but not many

Tombstone of Titus Annius who died '*in bello*' (*RIB* 3364).

'Street of Tombs' from Pompeii showing the disposition of tombs on the roads leading out of a Roman city. (CC-Public Domain 1.0)

tombstones survive. Cemeteries in the Roman world were located outside occupational areas and were usually found on the roads that led in and out of towns and cities (seen prominently at Pompeii in Italy), thus offering maximum visibility of monuments which advertise rank and status. At Vindolanda, the cemeteries have not yet been located and they probably lie to the west of the extramural settlement outside the area currently available for excavation. It is fortunate that this stone to Titus Annius was reused in a later building inside the fort, allowing us a glimpse of the deceased at Vindolanda.

42. Quintus Sollonius brooch (SF-9885)
Vindolanda Period 5 (*c*. CE 120–140)
Found in compressed floor levels of a workshop outside the fort
Disc diameter: 38mm; Pin plate: 38mm × 8mm

This extraordinary silver object is an excellent example of the attempts made by many to mark their belongings, found on expensive brooches such as this one, as well as the most mundane objects. It must have been a visiting legionary soldier who wore and lost this precious item on which had been punched the words 'Q. Sollonius, century of Cupitus'. We must presume that this implied it was the 'property of' the soldier. Unfortunately, it appears that the label did not help its owner recover his property. The brooch itself depicts the god Mars (now headless) in the centre with two standards and shields flanking. Three silver chains with leaf terminals at their ends dangle from the bottom. The shields depicted resemble those of the Dacians carved on the Column of Trajan in the centre of Rome, which may indicate that Quintus Sollonius served in the Dacian Wars (CE 101–106) and wore the brooch as a symbol of pride in his service and experiences.

We find the names of individuals scratched on many objects, not just items of precious metals. A pewter plate found on the floor of a Period 5 workshop (*c*. CE 120–140) inside the fort records the name of Annius Martialis, who scratched it into the surface of his property, presumably to keep it safe from loss or theft (SF-8321). Similarly, the most simple of Samian Ware cups are often found with the name of the owner scratched on the underside in an attempt to differentiate them from identical everyday items. The example opposite reads 'Mariani' in retrograde on the base of the cup, meaning it was the property 'of Marianus' (SF-9297).

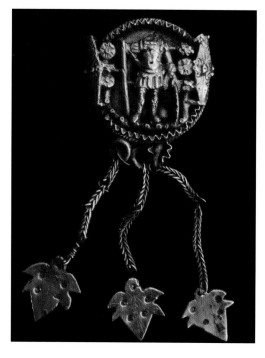

Silver brooch depicting Mars and inscribed with the name 'Q. Sollonius'.

0   10 cm

Pewter plate with a graffito recording the name 'Annius Martialis' (SF-8321).

Base of *terra sigillata* cup with the name 'Mariani' scratched in retrograde on the base (SF-9297).

0   10 cm

43. *Matri Patri* **finger ring (SF-10964)**
Vindolanda Period 7 (*c.* CE 213–275)
Found in the cobbled floor surface of a storage yard in the extramural settlement
Inner diameter: 17.5mm; Outer diameter: 19.4mm; Width of band: 5–8mm;
Band thickness: 1.4mm; Bezel face: 9 × 12mm

This fabulous silver finger ring, inscribed with the words '*Matri/Patri*', indicates a sense of longing for home and family. Although we cannot really know the owner's motivation, it seems likely that the inscribed words served as a sentimental reminder of home. The ability to express emotion, or perhaps nostalgia, through words indicates the power of writing in this context, where some people were quite mobile and perhaps stationed at Vindolanda for only a short period of time. Other finger rings in the collection express a similar sentimentality, such as the ring with the words '*anima mea*' inscribed on six faceted surfaces of a carnelian gemstone set into a gold bezel (SF-300; early third century CE). The phrase may have been a love token meaning something similar to 'my soul' or 'my darling'. Religious sentiments were also carved onto small objects such as rings and intaglios (gemstone settings), as on a silver ring with an inscription on the bezel reading MA/TRIBU/PARC, probably '*Matribu(s) Parc(is)*' meaning 'To the Mothers the Fates' (SF-6324; late first or early second century CE).

Above left: Finger ring with the words '*Matri Patri*' inscribed on the bezel.

Above right: Gold ring with a carnelian gemstone inscribed on six faces with the words '*anima mea*' (SF-300).

Finger ring with the abbreviated words for '*Matribus Parcis*' scratched on the round bezel (SF-6324).

44. Clepsydra fragment inscribed '*September*' (SF-12233)
Vindolanda Period 7–8 (*c.* third–fourth century CE)
Found in collapsed material south of the stone granaries inside Stone Fort 2
Length: 83mm; Width: 21mm

This fragment of a 'calendrical clepsydra' is one of only a handful of similar objects known in the Roman world. The word '*September*' is inscribed on its surface in full, as well as the letters K (standing for the first day of the month known as the *Kalends*), the letter N (short for the fifth day of the month called the *Nones*), and the letter I (marking the *Ides* which fall on the thirteenth of September). Also present is the abbreviation AE, marking the autumnal equinox (*Aequinoctium*). Each of these abbreviations sits beside a hole that would have been used to move a peg around the object, each hole representing a period of two days. This object functioned as both a calendar and a clock. Its use was not clear when it was first excavated in 2008, but a similar fragment from Hambledon, Hampshire and comparison to a complete example in the Archaeological Museum in Frankfurt (image below) allowed a more complete understanding of how it worked. Holes in the base of the bowl allowed the descending level of the water to mark twelve variable length hours of daylight and darkness throughout the year as they changed with the seasons, while the pegs moving around the rim of the bowl mark the months, days, and astronomical events such as equinoxes and solstices. The Vindolanda fragment is similar to other calendrical devices used in antiquity but is one of only three such devices currently known.

Fragment of a calendrical clepsydra recording the month of September and special days marked.

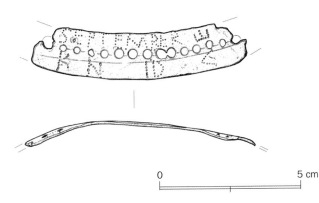

0   5 cm

Above left: Illustration of the Vindolanda clepsydra fragment. (M. Hoyle)

Above right: Example of a complete Clepsydra now in the Frankfurt Archaeological Museum. (inv.-nr.2000.7 Archäologisches Museum Frankurt)

Chapter 8
Animals in the Community

We should never underestimate the importance of animals in antiquity, from their role in agriculture and transport, to their function as pets, or their presence on the battlefield. Large animals were the vehicles of the ancient world and small animals served many similar purposes to those of today, as hunting partners or pets. Animals were associated symbolically with certain deities and they came to represent concepts such as fertility, good fortune, or strength. In the context of a military settlement we might think immediately

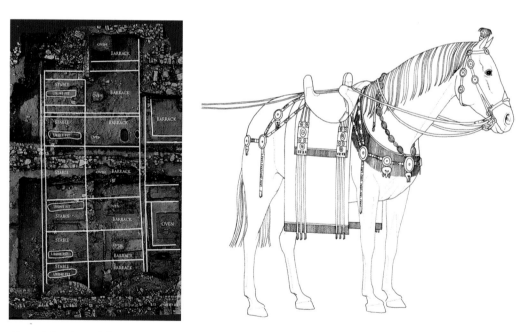

Above left: Plan of the Period 4 cavalry barracks laid over an aerial photo of the excavation of the area.

Above right: Illustration of a horse with equipment and tack from the Roman period. (M. C. Bishop)

Vindolanda horse figurine (SF-441) and the current logo for the Vindolanda Fort and Museum.

of the eagle's role as a symbol of the strength and power of the Roman army and the empire, or of the necessity for hundreds of horses to accompany a cavalry unit. Vindolanda holds an enormous amount of cavalry equipment in its collections, from saddle pieces, to chamfrons, and bronze decorative equipment. The role of horses in transporting people and goods would have been enormously important and, in many ways, life could not have operated in the way that it did without them. Even today, the logo of the Vindolanda Trust is based on the Roman horse figurine found in 1971 (SF-441).

Everyday interaction with animals probably occurred in more subtle ways. Canine pets were fairly common in this setting and other animals were probably kept by individual households. The representation of animals is quite common in the form of brooches, sculpture, and on incised gemstones, indicating that they held a special place in the world of humans. We also cannot forget their final contribution as a food source. Every year, the excavations at Vindolanda produce dozens of bags of cow, sheep, and pig bones that show extensive signs of butchery and preparation as a food source. Animals also provided all the leather that was used to produce the shoes, clothing, and equipment needed to stay warm and dry on the northern frontier. Tanning facilities must have existed nearby, though none have yet been discovered, and leather hides often entered the fort and appear in the official supply lists of the Roman army.

45. Decorated horse chamfron (L-1987-1345)
Vindolanda Period 3 (*c*. CE 100–105)
Found on the floor of Room XI of the *praetorium*
Length: 510mm; Width: 449mm; Depth: 6mm

Many of the military units stationed at Vindolanda were cavalry *alae* (or part-mounted units) and left behind a great deal of physical evidence of their horsemanship. One of the most beautiful cavalry objects to come from the collection is the almost complete chamfron, a ceremonial head mask for a horse, which has been closely examined by Carol van Driel-Murray. It is one of possibly seven or eight chamfrons to be found at Vindolanda. The chamfron is made of thick leather with a fine hide lining. Most of the studded decorations have not survived or were removed before deposition. A large round *phalera* (decorative plate) was fixed to the forehead and a separate panel, presumably with the name of the horse, the rider, and his unit, has been lost. Three small copper-alloy attachments in the shape of ivy leaves with faces of Bacchus remain attached. One attachment is missing and may have been used as a mould to manufacture new decorative elements. The Vindolanda chamfrons all show that the useful material was salvaged possibly for making new equipment before they were discarded. These objects would have been made-to-measure and offcuts fitting a similar pattern were found nearby.

Roman saddles have also been excavated, and a few fragments come from Vindolanda (L-1986-641). The object pictured opposite is a reconstruction of the most complete saddle fragment from the site, which provided the details that allowed for a full understanding of Roman saddles. The wear and stress put on the object is evident, resulting in conclusive proof that the Romans used a ridged saddle tree.

Replica of the Vindolanda chamfron with copper-alloy decorative elements.

Above: Illustration of the
Vindolanda chamfron.
(B. Browenstjin)

Right: Reconstruction of the
most complete Roman saddle
from Vindolanda (L-1986-641).
(P. Connolly)

46. Hipposandals (SF-21716 a-d)
Vindolanda Period 6A (*c.* CE 160–200)
Found in the fill at the top of a defensive fort ditch
Length: 188mm; Width: 105.4mm; Depth: 148.6mm

In 2018, four hipposandals, in sets of two, were found discarded in the fill of a defensive ditch. The Vindolanda collection only holds one other hipposandal which is in a much poorer condition. However, they are not uncommon elsewhere in Britain, especially in urban contexts. The most common theory about similar iron objects was that they were a type of horseshoe. They were not nailed to the hooves of a horse in the way modern horseshoes are, but rather were worn tied to horses' feet with cords made of organic materials. Hipposandals could be fitted by anyone who owned a horse, with little need for specialist farrier knowledge. All horses' gaits – especially trot, canter, and gallop – involve the four legs collecting close together under the body of the animal, either two-by-two on the ground or all four in the air. Any horse may have injured its own legs if manoeuvred at pace while wearing such heavy sandals. In fact, some researchers support the theory that hipposandals are not horseshoes at all; they argue that these objects could only have been used on slower pack animals such as oxen, mules, and donkeys. Other theories suggest that they were used as hobbles to stop the horse straying while grazing, to hold salves packed in or around the iron to heal hoof injuries, to help hooves avoid painful caltrops, or to offer better traction on ice and mud.

Set of hipposandals on display in the Roman Army Museum.

47. '*Fidelis*' tile with dog print (SF-19621)
Vindolanda Period 7 (*c.* CE 213–275)
Found in the rampart mound inside the fort
Length: 196mm; Width: 109mm; Depth: 51mm

The animals that roamed around the site of Vindolanda are clearly depicted in the numerous tiles with animal prints accidentally marked on their surface. Tiles were manufactured on-site and at least one kiln complex has been explored in an area to the north of the fort and settlement. During the production process, tiles were sometimes walked on by animals while they were drying before being fired in the kiln. We have evidence for dogs, cats, and cloven animals having traipsed through these manufacturing areas and left behind their footprints. This example is especially interesting because of the additional graffito that accompanied the paw print of a dog – the word *fidelis* (loyal) was found scratched into the tile after production and directly next to the paw print. Another dog named Fidelis is found in a mosaic from the town of Constantine in Algeria, in which a hunting dog helps herd antelope. This naming is quite emotive, considering our own modern association with dogs and their loyalty to humans, found in the name Fido. The presence of dogs on-site is also confirmed by the skeletal remains of different kinds of dogs found during excavations in all occupation periods. Images of dogs are also prominent in the objects on-site, including intaglios with canine hunting companions (SF-8474, see Object 49), a stone relief with a hare and hound depicted on its face (SF-19198), and a bronze handle in the shape of a hound (SF-10035, not pictured).

Roman tile with the word '*fidelis*' scratched into the surface next to the paw print of a dog.

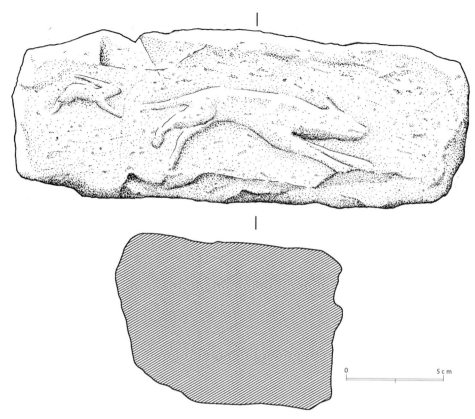

Illustration of the stone depicting a hare and hound chase (SF-19198). (M. Hoyle)

Almost complete skeleton of one of the Vindolanda dogs.

Brooches were used as more than just clothing fasteners in the Roman world, and zoomorphic brooches are an excellent example of this. Similar to other types of personal adornment, these animal-themed artefacts were often brightly coloured with enamels or of flamboyant design which would have been striking in contrast to the often comparatively drab cloth colours available to most people in the ancient world. It is hard to determine why an individual chose the animal they did for their brooches, and perhaps the brooch had no significance to the wearer other than aesthetic appeal. It is interesting to note that animals that were important in Romano-Celtic iconography are rarely found in this brooch type. The fantastic duck brooch seen here was discovered in 2018, after it was discarded or lost in a defensive fort ditch. It is made of silver and is in a style called *trompetenmunster,* or trumpet-scroll design. This motif is more abstract and even when it was found it was not immediately noted to be a duck. This stylised design is closely related to Celtic forms. It is thought that the duck was a symbol of honesty, simplicity, and resourcefulness, and because of their migratory nature they are associated with periods of transition.

Silver brooch in the form of a stylised duck.

49. Leopard pin (SF-5914)
Vindolanda Period 4 (*c.* CE 105–120)
Found in the large central timber structure inside the Period 4 fort
Total length: 130mm; Leopard terminal: 29 × 24mm, Depth: 8mm

Animals are found depicted on almost every type of object and, in this case, a detailed little leopard adorns the top of an iron pin. This object may have been used as a hairpin, but the leopard decoration appears a bit heavy for its successful operation in this way. The iron pin is somewhat incongruous to the relatively high quality of the copper-alloy leopard adorning the end. The object is quite elaborate with details of the fur etched onto the surface of the animal's body. The face is well rendered with mouth, snout, and eyes all clearly demarcated. The animal stands on a platform that rests on top of a feature resembling a column capital. There may not have been real meaning to the depiction of the animal except for the affinity humans have had with animals for thousands of years. We find similar representations on other decorative objects such as intaglios, which depict numerous animals. In the Vindolanda collection, gemstones display eagles, a scorpion, a cow, cockerels, dolphins, stags, a raven (SF-8649), and dogs (SF-8474). Animals are often associated with good luck or the expectation of success in activities such as hunting, and we can imagine that when one wore such a motif in any format it brought a perception of good fortune or luck to its owner.

Above left: Red jasper intaglio depicting Cupid hunting birds with his dog (SF-8474).

Above right: Agate intaglio depicting a raven feeding a smaller bird below its beak (SF-8649).

Left: Iron pin with a copper-alloy terminal in the shape of a small carved leopard.

50. Leather toy mouse (L-1993-4131)
Vindolanda Period 3 (*c.* CE 100–105)
Found in a timber structure inside the fort
Length: 120mm; Width: 28mm; Depth: 3mm

This small piece of leather was cut and decorated to look like a mouse and was possibly used as a soft toy by a small child. The shape of the piece is quite deliberate with four legs and a roughly triangular head with a pointed nose, in the way mice are commonly depicted. The tail is long and bends slightly, and the surface of the leather has even been etched with stylised marks representing fur. There is nothing else like this in the leather assemblage, and it is quite different from the manufacturing offcuts and leather scraps that are abundant in the collection. Children's play objects are found throughout the Roman world, including in burials of girls and boys. Toys such as dolls and wooden swords and daggers (see Object 13) demonstrate ideals about gender expectations and education of children. These objects are not common but the large number of shoes at Vindolanda that demonstrate the presence of children throughout all periods of settlement suggest that more toys will be found to further illuminate our understanding of children's play in antiquity.

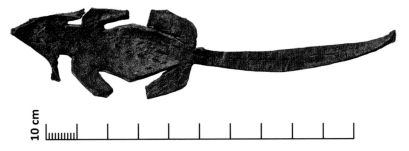

Above: Small leather scrap fashioned into the shape of a mouse.

Right: Drawing of the leather mouse 'toy' found in a pile of offcuts.

Bibliography and Further Resources

Digital Resources for Vindolanda Material

Complete bibliography of publications on Vindolanda and recent research blogs: vindolanda.com/research

Vindolanda excavation reports: vindolanda.com/excavation-reports

Visiting the site of Vindolanda: vindolanda.com

Visiting the Roman Army Museum and Magna Roman Fort: romanarmymuseum.com

Visiting Hadrian's Wall Country: hadrianswallcountry.co.uk

The Vindolanda writing tablets (Roman Inscriptions of Britain Online): romaninscriptionsofbritain.org/inscriptions

Further Reading by Chapter

1. The Roman Fort at Vindolanda, the Army, and the Soldiers

Alberti, M. and M. C. Bishop, 'Three new swords from Vindolanda', *Journal of Roman Military Equipment Studies* 20 (2019), 103–13

Birley, Andrew, *The Excavations of 2001 and 2002* (The Vindolanda Trust, 2003)

Birley, Anthony R., *Garrison Life at Vindolanda: A Band of Brothers* (Tempus, 2002)

Birley, Robin, *The Making of Modern Vindolanda, with the Life and Work of Anthony Hedley 1777–1835* (Roman Army Museum Publications, 1995)

Birley, Robin, *Vindolanda: A Roman Frontier Fort on Hadrian's Wall* (Amberley Publishing, 2009)

Bishop, M. C., *The Gladius. The Roman Short Sword* (Osprey Publishing, 2016)

Bowman, A. K. and J. D. Thomas, 'A Military Strength Report from Vindolanda', *Journal of Roman Studies* 81 (1991), 62–73

Driel-Murray, C. van, J. P. Wild, M. Seaward, J. Hillam, *Vindolanda Research Reports New Series. Volume III. The Early Wooden Forts: Preliminary Reports on the Leather, Textiles, Environmental Evidence and Dendrochronology* (Roman Army Museum Publications, 1993)

Goldsworthy, A., *The Complete Roman Army* (Thames & Hudson, 2011)

2. Women and Children at Vindolanda

Allason-Jones, L., 'Women and the Roman Army in Britain' in A. Goldsworthy and I. Haynes (eds), *The Roman Army as a Community* (Journal of Roman Archaeology, 1999), 41–51

Allason-Jones, L., *Jet, shale and other allied materials* (Roman Finds Group, Datasheet 2, 2011)

Allison, P. M., *People and Spaces in Roman Military Bases* (Cambridge University Press, 2013)

Allison, P. M., 'Soldiers' Families in the Early Roman Empire' in B. Rawson (ed.), *A Companion to Families in the Greek and Roman Worlds* (Wiley-Blackwell, 2011), 161–82

Birley, Robin, *Civilians on Rome's Northern Frontier: Families, Friends and Foes* (The Vindolanda Trust, 2000)

Dolansky, F., 'Roman girls and boys at play: Realities and representations' in C. Laes and V. Vuolanto (eds), *Children and Everyday Life in the Roman and Late Antique World* (Routledge, 2017), 116–36

Dolansky, F., 'Different Lives: Children's Daily Experiences in the Roman World' in L. Beaumont, M. Dillon, and N. Harrington (eds), *Childhood in Antiquity: Perspectives and Experiences of Childhood in the Ancient Mediterranean* (Routledge, 2021), 244–57

Driel-Murray, C. van, 'A question of gender in a military context', *Helinium* 34 (1994, 1998), 342–62

Greene, E. M., 'Female Networks in the Military Communities of the Roman West: A view from the Vindolanda Tablets' in E. Hemelrijk and G. Woolf (eds), *Women and the Roman City in the Latin West* (Brill, 2013), 369–90

Greene, E. M., 'Before Hadrian's Wall: Early military communities on the Roman frontier in Britain' in R. Collins and M. F. A. Symonds (eds), *Breaking Down Boundaries: Hadrian's Wall in the 21st Century* (Journal of Roman Archaeology, 2013), 17–32

Greene, E. M., 'Identities and Social Roles of Women in Military Communities of the Roman West' in S. Budin and J. Turfa (eds), *Women in Antiquity: Real Women across the Ancient World* (Routledge, 2016), 942–53

3. Religion and Worship in Roman Military Communities

Aldhouse-Green, M., *Sacred Britannia: The Gods and Rituals of Roman Britain* (Thames & Hudson, 2023)

Bédoyère, G., *The Finds of Roman Britain* (Batsford, 1989)

Birley, Andrew and M. Alberti, *Vindolanda Excavation Research Report. Focusing on Post-Roman Vindolanda* (The Vindolanda Trust, 2021)

Birley, Andrew and Anthony Birley, 'A new Dolichenum, inside the Third-century fort at Vindolanda' in M. Blömer and E. Winter (eds), *Iuppiter Dolichenus: Vom lokalkult zur Reichsreligion* (Mohr Siebeck, 2012), 231–57

Birley, Anthony R., Andrew Birley, and P. de Bernardo Stempel, 'A Dedication by the "Cohors I Tungrorum" at Vindolanda to a Hitherto Unknown Goddess', *Zeitschrift für Papyrologie und Epigraphik* 186 (2013), 287–300

Birley, Anthony R., 'Some Germanic deities and their worshippers in the British frontier zone' in H. Börm, N. Ehrhardt and J. Wiesehöfer (eds), *Monumentum et Instrumentum Inscriptum* (Franz Steiner, 2008), 31–46

Colins, R., *Living on the edge of Empire, the objects and people of Hadrian's Wall* (Pen & Sword, 2020)

Collins, R. and R. Sands, 'Touch wood: Luck, protection, power or pleasure? A wooden phallus from Vindolanda Roman fort', *Antiquity* (2023), 1–17

Henig, M., *Religion in Roman Britain* (Routledge, 1984)

Irby-Massie, G. L., *Military Religion in Roman Britain* (Brill, 1999)

4. Dress, Adornment, and the Body

Birley, Barbara and E. Greene, *The Roman Jewellery from Vindolanda* (The Vindolanda Trust, 2006)

Cool, H. E. M., 'Clothing and Identity' in M. Millett, L. Revell, and A. Moore (eds), *The Oxford Handbook of Roman Britain* (Oxford University Press, 2014), 406–24

Sumner, G., *Roman Military Dress* (The History Press, 2009)

Johns, C., *The Jewellery of Roman Britain, Celtic and Classical Traditions* (Routledge, 1996)

Rothe, U., 'Dress and cultural identity in the Roman Empire' in M. Harlow (ed.), *Dress and Identity* (Archaeopress, 2012), 59–68

Rothe, U., 'Whose fashion? Men, women and Roman culture as reflected in dress in the cities of the Roman north-west' in E. Hemelrijk and G. Woolf (eds), *Women and the Roman City in the Latin West* (Brill, 2013), 243–68

Wild, J. P., 'Vindolanda 1985–1988: The Textiles' in C. van Driel-Murray, J. P. Wild, M. Seaward, J. Hillam, *Vindolanda Research Reports New Series. Volume III. The Early Wooden Forts: Preliminary Reports on the Leather, Textiles, Environmental Evidence and Dendrochronology* (Roman Army Museum Publications, 1993), 76–90

5. Economy, Trade, and Industry on the Frontier

Birley, Andrew, *Security: The Keys and Locks. Vindolanda Research Report New Series. Volume IV. Small Finds Fascicule II* (Roman Army Museum Publications, 1997)

Birley, Anthony, *Coins of the Roman Emperors Found at Vindolanda* (Roman Army Museum Publications, 2015)

Birley, Robin, *Vindolanda Research Reports, New Series. Volume 1: The Early Wooden Forts* (Roman Army Museum Publications, 1994)

Blake, J., *The Tools. Vindolanda Research Reports, New Series. Volume IV, Fascicule III* (Roman Army Museum Publications, 1999)

Erdkamp, P. (ed.), *The Roman Army and the Economy* (J. C. Gieben, 2002)

Evers, K. G., *The Vindolanda Tablets and the Ancient Economy* (British Archaeological Reports, 2011)

Harvey, C. A. and E. M. Greene, 'The newly excavated brick and tile kiln in the Vindolanda North Field' in H. Van Enckevort, M. Driessen, E. Graafstal, T. Hazenberg, T. Ivleva and C. van Driel-Murray (eds), *Supplying the Roman Army: Proceedings of the 25th International Congress of Frontier Studies*, Vol. 4 (Sidestone Press, 2024), 213–20

Whittaker, C. R., 'Supplying the Army: Evidence from Vindolanda' in P. Erdkamp (ed.), *The Roman Army and the Economy* (J. C. Gieben, 2002), 204–34

6. Recreation and Leisure

Birley, Andrew, 'Boxing for the Roman Empire, the Gloves are Off' in W. Eck, F. Santangelo, and K. Vössing (eds), *Emperor, Army and Society: Studies in Roman Imperial History for Anthony R. Birley* (Rudolf Habelt, 2022), 3–16

Birley, A. and J. Blake, *Vindolanda Excavations 2003–2004* (The Vindolanda Trust, 2005)

Campbell, L., 'The Vindolanda Vessel: pXRF and Microphotography of an Enamel-Painted Roman Gladiator Glass', *Heritage* 6 (2023), 3638–3672

Courts, S. and T. Penn, *Roman gaming boards from Britain* (Roman Finds Group, Datasheet 13, 2021)

Hoss, S. (ed.), *Latrinae: Roman Toilets in the Northwestern Provinces of the Roman Empire* (Archaeopress, 2018)

Sands, R. and J. A. Horn, 'Bring me three large beers: Wooden tankards at Roman Vindolanda', *Oxford Journal of Archaeology* 36.1 (2017), 71–83

Sands, R. and E. Marlière, 'Produce, Repair, Reuse, Adapt, and Recycle: The multiple biographies of a Roman barrel', *European Journal of Archaeology* (2020), 1–25

7. The Power of Words and Writing

Birley, Anthony R., 'A new tombstone from Vindolanda', *Britannia* 29, 299–306

Birley, Andrew and J. Blake, *Vindolanda Research Report. The Excavations of 2005-2006* (The Vindolanda Trust, 1998, 2007)

Birley, Eric, Robin Birley and Anthony R. Birley, *Vindolanda Research Report, New Series, Volume II. The Early Wooden Forts: Reports on the Auxiliaries, writing tablets, inscriptions, brands and graffiti* (Roman Army Museum Publications, 1993)

Birley, Robin, *Vindolanda: Extraordinary Records of Daily Life on the Northern Frontier* (Roman Army Museum Publications, 2005)

Birth, K., 'The Vindolanda Timepiece: Time and Calendar Reckoning in Roman Britain', *Oxford Journal of Archaeology* 33.4 (2014), 395–411

Bowman, A. K., *Life and Letters on the Roman Frontier: Vindolanda and its People*, 3rd edn (Routledge, 2003)

Bowman, A. K. and J. D. Thomas, *The Vindolanda Writing-Tablets: Tabulae Vindolandenses Volume II* (The British Museum Press, 1994)

Bowman, A. K. and J. D. Thomas, *The Vindolanda Writing-Tablets: Tabulae Vindolandenses Volume III* (The British Museum Press, 2003)

Dolansky, F., 'Education in the Roman World' in M. Gibbs and M. Nikolic, with P. Ripat (eds), *Themes in Roman Society and Culture: An Introduction to Ancient Rome*, 2nd edn (Oxford University Press, 2020), 179–99

Meyer, A., 'The Vindolanda Calendrical Clepsydra: Time-Keeping and Healing Waters', *Britannia* 50 (2019), 185–202

Meyer, A., A. Mullen, and J. Vanhala, 'A Scato-sexual Message: The Secundinus Stone with Phallus from Vindolanda', *Britannia* (2023), 1–16. doi: doi.org/10.1017/S0068113X2300020X

Mullen, A., 'Socio-literacy: an interdisciplinary approach to understanding literacy in the Roman North-West' in M. Ramírez and N. Moncunill (eds), *Aprender la escritura, olvidar la escritura* (Vitoria, 2021), 357–80

Tomlin, R. S. O., 'Literacy in Roman Britain' in A. Kolb (ed.), *Literacy in Ancient Everyday Life* (Walter de Gruyter, 2018), 201–19

Willi, A., 'Inscriptions for inscribers: texts on Roman writing equipment', *Journal of Epigraphic Studies* 5 (2022), 63–104

Willi, A., *Manual of Roman Everyday Writing Vol. 2 Writing Equipment* (LatinNow ePubs, Nottingham, 2021) (interactive e-book)

8. Animals in the Community

Bennett, D. and R. M. Timm, 'Dogs of Roman Vindolanda, Part IV: Large sighthounds and guard and utility dogs', *Archaeofauna* 30 (2021), 185–216 (see also articles on Vindolanda dog skeletons in *Archaeofauna* volumes 25 and 27)

Connolly, P. and C. van Driel-Murray, 'The Roman Cavalry Saddle', *Britannia* 22 (1991), 33–50

Driel-Murray, C. van, 'The Vindolanda chamfrons and miscellaneous items of leather horse gear', *Roman military equipment. The sources of evidence. Proceedings of the Fifth Roman Military Equipment Conference* (British Archaeological Reports, 1989), 281–318

Huntley, J., '"The World is a bundle of hay": Investigating land management for animal fodder around Vindolanda, based on plant remains' in R. Collins and M. Symonds (eds), *Breaking Down Boundaries, Hadrian's Wall in the 21st Century* (Journal of Roman Archaeology, 2013), 33–52

Smith, I., *Vindolanda Roman Fort, Northumberland: Analysis of a fourth-century animal-bone assemblage* (Oxford Archaeology North, 2021)

Toynbee, J. M. C. and Alan Wilkins, 'The Vindolanda Horse', *Britannia* 13 (1982), 245–51

Toynbee, J. M. C., 'Beasts and their names in the Roman empire', *Papers of the British School at Rome* 16 (1948), 24–37